Practical Religion

By

Stephen W. Ervin

AmErica House
Baltimore

2001 by Stephen W. Ervin.

First printing

ISBN: 1-58851-238-X
PUBLISHED BY AMERICA HOUSE BOOK
PUBLISHERS
www.publishamerica.com
Baltimore

Printed in the United States of America

CHAPTER 1

Searching for the Truth

If you ask the question, "Is there a God? where would you go to get the answer? No matter who you go to, your parents, your minister, your political representative, you hear the familiar words, "You gotta have faith! Another favorite of those who do not really have the answer is, "God always was, and always will be. These answers provoke the question, "How can it be known for sure whether a God exists or not? Similar questions that seem to pop up are "Did God really complete earth in seven days? Did he really create the Universe, earth, and man? What about the "big bang theory? Is man really an animal that evolved from ape like creatures? What are UFOs? Is there other intelligent life in the Universe? Is there to be an end of the world? Is Jesus really the Savior of man? In asking all these various questions, a person is really asking one single question, "What is the absolute truth about everything?

The world has long suffered under the burden of everything but the truth, and this calamity comes from two sources: man himself, and Satan. In order to start some type evaluation, a person must first come to understand the ingredients that serve to make up information, and how they affect each of us. The evaluation starts with the simple premise that a person's philosophy is based upon what the person believes is the absolute truth. In this, there are those who correctly believe, and those whose belief is flawed or in error. Both camps believe they are correct in their belief. This makes the rule that man's philosophy is based on what the individual believes to be the absolute truth. Because there are those who are right and those who are wrong in their assessment, two different patterns and standards of behavior are fact. It can be said that behavior is the reflection of the philosophy, because behavior, a person's actions, is determined by what he thinks.

This can be narrowed to two basics beliefs. One is the belief in God, and the other is the belief that no God exists. Those who believe a God exists are called religious, and those who do not believe a God exist are called atheists. The world is divided into these two general groups and this divides man's philosophy and behavior into two groups.

Those who believe in God, are bound by the ethics of his words, and are called spiritually minded. Those who are atheist are bound to physical instincts and are called earthy. Each group uses information they regard as the absolute truth as the basis of their belief. The religious use ancient documents and artifacts to support their belief, and the atheist uses scientific theory and physical evidence to support their belief.

It is obvious that only one can be correct, because they are in opposition to one another. In being so, part of the world is correct in their belief, and part of the world is wrong in their belief. Which is right, and which is wrong? That can only be decided by looking at all the offered information, and sorting it out to a degree which becomes factual, logical, and right. This can only be done by using absolute truth as the basis of our philosophy and building on it as new facts come to light.

Absolute truth is defined as that which is fact, that which is logical, and that which is right. Absolute untruth is that which is not fact, that which is illogical, and that which is wrong. The best way to demonstrate the effect is to take a blank sheet of paper and draw a line across the page. Label the left end of the line Absolute Truth, and under it list the attributes, fact, logical, right. Label the right end of the line Absolute Untruth, and under it list the attributes, not fact, illogical, and wrong. It can be seen, that between the two ends, there is a large part of the line without a title, and this section is to be labeled Perceived Truth and its definition is information that lacks one or more attributes of absolute truth. For this reason, perceived truth may seem to be correct, when it is not.

Most of the information we receive is perceived truth, and should not be used to alter, amend, or change the foundation of our philosophy. Such a change should be initiated only after determining the new information is the absolute truth and that it is in conflict with the presently held convictions. The erratic behavior of people in the world today can be attributed to having a muddled philosophy, one based on uncertain beliefs, and producing uncertain behavior.

The two major beliefs in the world today are the religious, and the atheist. The religious are subdivided into religions. There are eleven great religions on earth today, and in each there are sects or divisions who practice the religion in their own way, but hold fast to the foundation or root belief. The best example is the many denominations of the Christian religion. The root belief is in Jesus Christ, but each denomination worship in different rites and ceremonies.

Of the eleven great religions, only the Islamic, Judaic, and Christian religions believe in monotheism, one God. The others have a set of codes, ethics, and deities which govern them.

While the atheist denies a God exists, there is the element called agnostics which say a God might exist, but stoutly maintain it has never been adequately proven. The agnostic is more aligned with the atheist than with the religious.

In the very basic, each person on earth has to decide which way to believe, and it becomes apparent that instruction determines the outcome. Instruction is the assimilation of information, and knowledge is the result. Wisdom is the result of having discarded information proven false, and retaining that proven true. It is then practical to clean house, stripping out that which is not fact, illogical and wrong, and retaining the information proven to be factual, logical and right, in other words, the absolute truth.

Two important observations can be made. The first is that because of how much information a person is exposed to, the rate of repetition, and the duration of the repetitive message, all people become deceived to some degree. This means that each person has some false information located in their philosophy, and since behavior is contingent upon philosophy, each person's behavior is also flawed to some degree. This is what makes each person a individual. It can be said an individual reflects in behavior, the environment he is subjected to. This physical reaction can be overcome by spiritual perseverance in the group who believe in God.

One way perceived truth can be detected is to discover its purpose, and it can be said with reasonable accuracy that perceived truth, information lacking one or more elements of absolute truth, is used to deceive people. The motive for deceiving people is varied, and can range from wanting you to buy one product over another, or to convince you to believe a specific way.

Here's an example of simple deception to induce a person to buy one product over another. On the supermarket shelves is a display of red and yellow spray cans, and on the can is emblazoned, "33% MORE FREE! The first impression is that in buying this product you will receive about one third more for the same money, and that seems like a good buy. You can relate that if you were talking about a dozen eggs, this would be four more eggs for the same price, and would be a good buy. It is only when you read the label of the can that the absolute truth comes across. The list of ingredients read, 1% active ingredients 99% inactive ingredients. The 1% is the product, and the 99% is the propellant. The 33% increase is of the same ratio, and is obtained by a tiny increase in pressure in the can, increasing the volume in the can. True the can does contain 33% more volume, but the actual benefit is negligible, because 33% of 1% (the active ingredient) is negligible. On another shelf might be a product with 2% active ingredients for about the same money, and would be a better buy. The innuendo of the advertising is to get you to buy the particular product over another, and the ruse works very effectively on those who do not give sufficient attention to comparing products.

Another example is the new car rebate. Few average wage earners can come up with the required down payment for a new car, so the manufacturer, dealer, and lending institutions have devised the new car rebate to allow the average person to buy a car with virtually nothing down. The car is overpriced by the manufacturer from a few hundred to thousands of dollars, and then this excess is used as a rebate, and used as the down payment. In this way, the average person can purchase a new car for nothing down, and it seems like a good deal, which it is for the dealer, the manufacturer, and the financial institution, but the consumer gets hit with interest on a higher amount financed, length of time payments, and an immediate loss of value of the car by the face amount of the rebate, plus normal loss of value incurred by the car becoming a used car, even though it has never been driven. The book used by dealers for trade in value, never equals the new car price. In the case of a cash buy the rebate becomes a marking down tool by the dealer, so the cash buyer gets to buy the car at an actual small discount, which looks big when considering the rebate.

In advertising such deception is called "fluff and seems innocent enough, until a person begins to accept such nonsense as the truth. The rule about this is that the more deceived you are, the more you will be. Some call it gullible, some say it's stupidity, and some have cute little remarks and witty sayings about those deceived, like, "His car doesn't go to the top floor! He doesn't have enough sense to come in out of the rain! and other such witticisms. The young, the very old, and the unknowing all fall victim to cleverly devised and disguised schemes to deceive, and the biggest perpetrator of this deception comes from agencies people trust. Science, government at all levels, education, and commerce have become the biggest source of deception on the face of the earth, and it doesn't matter in which country or nation you happen to be living in. The fact is clear, the major agencies people rely most on are the biggest liars in the world!

Science has adopted the theory of evolution as the reason why and how life came to be on the planet. They classify man as an animal of the mammal family and distantly related to the chimpanzee, the apes, and the monkeys. To the scientist there is only the physical life, the same as the life of any animal, and to destroy the life of a person is no different than taking the life of any other animal. In this dissertation, man operates on instinctive behavior, the same as any other animal, and therefore any behavior is natural in the "survival of the fittest regimen.

When science got around to classifying things on earth, it used three broad categories, Plant, Animal, and Mineral. Man was lumped into the animal classification because to admit that man was more than an animal would destroy the theory of evolution, and the belief in atheism. Science then had to continue to lie about their its discoveries in order to maintain the theory of evolution, and the atheist belief.

Part of the problem comes from the two major premises science uses in discovering evidence. The first premise is, "Even if the information is wrong, the truth will eventually emerge. This is like saying that after so many failures there has to come success. Try as one might to make water run up hill, it won't, and to persist in trying to make it run up hill is futile, and so is trying to get the truth to come out of something false. It just can't be done.

The second premise science uses is that evolution alone explains life on the planet, and the "big bang theory explains how the Universe came into existence. This premise is used in every bit of correspondence and information coming out of science today, despite what is known and proven true. It is designed to convey the atheist belief.

Government, because it relies on scientific information and findings slanted to atheism, has become atheist in practice, because it follows the lead of science. There is no government on earth that practices spiritual leadership because every government is designed to control the physical presence that is recognized as life. No government recognizes the spiritual life of man, and promotes spirituality above the physical expression of life. For that reason, no government is other than atheist in belief. It will not be until Christ returns to earth that spiritual life and spiritual government will become actuality.

Education, under the control of governmental bodies and reliance on science for information, teaches the theory of evolution, the big bang theory, and other suppositions as the absolute truth, and is made atheist in practice because of what is taught the students

All commerce is based upon greed, and greed is in opposition to what God and Christ teaches as ethical. Greed is the accumulation of physical things over and above what is needed to sustain life. Under this definition, the beggar would be the only person living to the ethic, if it were not softened by God's word of prosperity, which means in abundance to bring spiritual joy. A person with adequate food, clothing, shelter, and other necessary things in life, can afford to turn his thoughts to being spiritual, and God knows this. All commerce is dedicated to the gathering of physical wealth, and has to be classified as greed, and greed is an exaggeration of prosperity.

The four major divisions of society play a huge part in the everyday lives of the population of earth, and what they peddle as the truth is consumed by the masses of people, because the people believe these agencies are above lying, or giving out false information.

The question arises, "If science, government, education and commerce can't be trusted to give out the truth, where is the truth to be found? To discover the absolute truth the source of where information is stored has to be looked at. Who hasn't been taught to use the encyclopedia as an authoritative reference? School, government, private industry, and private citizens all use this source of information as the source of absolute truth, but is it?

The encyclopedia is a set of books arranged alphabetically, and contains information on nearly every subject known to man. The initial issue is about thirty books, and each year an annual or year book is issued to update the basic set with the latest findings of scientists. After ten or more years, when it has become too cumbersome to cross reference between the year books and the basic set, the basic set is revised using the latest material available and the system starts over. What can be said about the encyclopedia is this. What was read in the basic books is not the truth because it is amended by what is written in the yearbook or annual. What is written in the yearbook or annual isn't the truth because the material is revised by subsequent yearbooks or annuals. From this standpoint, the encyclopedia has to be classified as perceived truth, having some merit, but should not be used in place of absolute truth.

There is a source of absolute truth in the world today and it, too, is a collection of books, but these books are incorporated under one cover, and is called the Holy Bible. Because the Holy Bible is the absolute truth, there is no need or requirement to revise it. Those who would attempt to change the Holy Bible are warned in the book of Revelation 22:18 and 19, of the punishment of such revision. "For I testify unto every man that heareth the words of the prophecy of this book, if any man shall add unto these things, God shall add unto him the plagues that are written in this book: And if any man shall take away from the words of the book of this prophecy, God shall take away his part out of the book of life, and from the things which are written in this book.

For those unaccustomed to Biblical scripture, Revelation is the book, 22 is the chapter in the book, and 18 and 19 are the two verses quoted. It is recommended the King James Version (KJV) of the Holy Bible be used, as other versions may vary in word usage and intent, having previously been interpreted and slanted.

Why is the Holy Bible the only source of absolute truth in the world? The answer is that the Holy Bible is the word of God, and there is a lot of confusion about this, even in religious circles.

In a recent poll conducted by different churches, among people attending church on a regular basis, and who were asked, "Do you believe the Holy Bible to be the word of God? came these responses. One third of those polled said they believed the Holy Bible was God's word to man. Two thirds said they believed the Holy Bible was man's interpretation of God's word. It can be seen by the results of the poll there is a wide difference of opinion, and again only one of the two can be correct in their assessment. 'Me answer is found in II Peter 1:20, and 21, "Knowing this first, that no prophecy of the scripture is of any private interpretation. For the prophecy came not in old time by the will of man: but holy men of God spake as they were moved by the Holy Ghost.

For those doubting how this could be achieved in a practical manner, the testimony in Jeremiah has to be taken into consideration. Jeremiah has just been told by God that he is to be a prophet unto the nations, and Jeremiah responds in Jeremiah 1:6, "Then said I, Ah, Lord God! I cannot speak: for I am a child. Jeremiah isn't any different from any other person, and what he's saying to God is, "Look God, there isn't any way I can talk for you, because I don't have the slightest notion or ability to know your mind! " Isn't that common in most people? Very few would go out on a limb to talk on a subject they know nothing about.

Jeremiah 1:7, "But the Lord said unto me, Say not I am a child: for thou shalt go to all that I shall send thee, and whatsoever I command thee thou shalt speak. It is made clear that Jeremiah isn't going to speak his own words, but the word of God. This is made even clearer in verse 9, "Then the Lord put forth his hand, and touched my mouth. And the Lord said unto me, Behold I have put my words in thy mouth. Can it be said any clearer that this?

For those still unconvinced, look at what is recorded in the other books of the prophets. In Ezekiel 1:3 is written, "The word of the Lord came expressly unto Ezekiel the priest. Then in Hosea 1: 1 is recorded, "The word of the Lord that came unto Hosea. In Joel 1: 1 is written, "The word of the Lord that came to Joel.... Again in Jonah 1: 1 is recorded, "Now the word of the Lord came unto Jonah.... And in Micah 1: 1 is written, "The word of the Lord that came to Micah.... These quotes serve as ample evidence that these prophets spoke not of their own volition, but spoke the word of God as they were moved to do so by the Holy Ghost. It also should put to an end of who is the actual author of the Holy Bible.

In the beginning, God walked with Adam, and so the absolute truth was known on earth by God's presence, and God taught Adam absolute truth. Christ walked among men, and he too brought the absolute truth to men, so man was again exposed to the absolute truth. That is in the past history of man, and now God has given man the absolute truth in the Holy Bible, because he no longer walks among man, and Christ no longer walks among man, and this means the Holy Bible is the only source of absolute truth in the world today.

The Holy Bible has been criticized as being contradictory, and this has to come from those not well versed in the Holy Bible. The Holy Bible is man's handbook to live a good physical life, and to have immortality in his spiritual life until sufficiently schooled by God and Christ to be like them. At that time, those found worthy will don immortality in both the spiritual and physical form.

There is a lot of mystery, intrigue, and misunderstanding about the Holy Bible, and these need explaining. The first concept is that the average person is too dumb to comprehend the wording in the Holy Bible, and therefore scholars, and others have to interpret the Holy Bible for you. This is pure fantasy. The Holy Bible is written so that any person who can read, can read a verse, sit back and reflect upon it, and while he is doing this, the Holy Ghost will impart to him the real, and hidden meaning of the verse. This means each verse has many meanings, and only the Holy Ghost is equipped to impart to you the knowledge of the verse for any given instance or incident. Whatever others tell you about a specific verse is only their interpretation at the moment, and may not apply to you. It is therefore impossible for man to successfully interpret the words of the Holy Bible without being guided to a successful conclusion by the Holy Ghost.

The reading, understanding, and inspiration of the Holy Bible is contingent upon each person's personal instruction by the Holy Ghost, and this makes the Holy Bible each person's personal handbook toward living. The book is designed and written in such a manner, that if the thread of truth is followed, verse to verse, book to book, eventually the whole book, and every verse is read and understood. Here is both the word of God, and an example of how the Holy Bible should be used.

It starts in Isaiah 28:9 and 10, "Whom shall he teach knowledge? and whom shall he make to understand doctrine? them that are weaned from the milk, and drawn from the breasts. There are two times we are weaned from the milk and drawn from the breasts. About the time we learn to drink from a glass, we are weaned from mother's milk, and put on cow's milk, and we're no longer suckled by our mother. It is at this time in our life, when we should begin to learn the word of God, simple things of right and wrong, but each lesson enforced from the view point of the Holy Bible. No child is going to grow up spiritually if he is not instructed in spiritual rights and wrongs, good and evil things. The body will mature, and the child will gain, as a result of aging, better survival skills, but spiritually if he is not taught, he will remain an infant. This is why it is important to teach Biblical views, and live Biblical ethics. The key is this. All civility is based upon the ethics of the Holy Bible and without civility there can be no harmony among people. The key to happiness, prosperity, and goodness lies in the reading, digesting, and applying that which we are instructed in the Holy Bible, and reinforced spiritually by the Holy Ghost.

Here is an example. The physical body is used to set all standards of life, but that is in conflict with what is written in the Holy Bible. This is where the second meaning of the verse comes in. When it is discovered that the world isn't all that it's supposed to be, most people start searching for something better, something that will fill the void in their life and being. They don't know what it is they are searching for, but they search. Unfortunately, the unhealthy and addiction habits are the ones that gain. Drugs, alcohol, promiscuous sex, smoking, over eating, and every other derelict behavior is the result of a failed search. What these people are searching for is the truth, and the only place the absolute truth can be found is in the Holy Bible.

It has been said, "The truth will set you free. Many people recite this verse, without benefit of knowing where the verse came from or what the full extent of the verse means. It is found in John 8:32, when Jesus was addressing a group of Jews, he said, "And ye shall know the truth, and the truth shall make you free. It is known that there is a release from fear whenever the truth is found, and that is part of what Christ said, but further more he was saying that he is the Truth, and by his sacrifice, man would be made free.

By using the physical body as the only reference point of life, we are in effect negating the truth as given man by God and Christ. Here's why. Science in the pure form of atheism says that life evolved on the planet, and that at some point in time, man evolved from single celled animals, like the amoebae to something like an ape, then prehistoric man, and finally modern man. From this atheist view there is no agreement between the theory of evolution and the truth of the Holy Bible.

In Genesis 1:26 is recorded, "And God said, Let us make man in our image, after our likeness.... This means man is physical in looks like God and when we look into a mirror we see our image, but moreover we are looking at the image of God because we are in his image. Therefore, it can be reasoned quite simply that when we cast disparaging remarks about another person's looks we are, in fact, casting disparaging remarks about God's looks, because each and every person is in the image of God. This is something new for a person to think about!

Being in the image of God explains our physical attributes, and this leads to the question, if man is in the image of God, and if man is an animal as theorized by science, is it not then logical to believe that God is an animal? The resolution to the question is that since God in no way can be compared to an animal, and since man is in God's image, he also cannot be an animal. Who would dare say God is an animal?

The fact is man is created in the image and likeness of God, and that means we physically look like God, and we have God's spiritual aspect as well. If we are replicas of God, then we are his offspring, and if we are his offspring we are his children, and if we are his children we are God like and not animal like. Doesn't this make more sense and easier to understand?

When God said we were created in his likeness, he meant having the Spirit of God dwelling in us, and that means we are unique in the whole Universe. It also raises many questions that have to be answered, and to get down to reasoning it out, we begin in Genesis 2:7, "And the Lord God formed man of the dust of the ground, and breathed into his nostrils the breath of life, and man became a living soul. There's a lot of misunderstanding about this verse. The truth is in the scientific knowledge that man is worth a few dollars in mineral content, and this substantiates man is of the earth. When God breathed into Adam's nostrils, he not only inflated Adam's lungs, even as CPR is used today, but he imparted to Adam, a bit of his own spirit, and Adam became a living spirit as well as being a physical being. This is man's uniqueness, he is half physical and he is half spiritual.

This uniqueness isn't just a happenstance occurrence, but a planned event dating back to the time before the Universe or earth was created by God. Look at what is recorded in Isaiah 43:7, "Even everyone that is called by my name: for I have created him for my glory. I have formed him; yea, I have made him. God doesn't just bring people into reality for a whim, but each person is known spiritually by God before they are born, and they are here on earth to add to God's glory by doing whatever God appoints them to do. The trouble is few, very few, ever awaken to the call God has put out to them. Christ reiterated this in Matthew 22:14, "For many are called; but few are chosen. Each person has to evaluate himself, and ask, "What is it I'm supposed to do for God while I am on earth?

It isn't mere coincidence there are great masters in art, music, and literature. Neither is it just by chance that these old masters realized their expression wasn't of their own, but inspiration given by God. It doesn't take much rationalization to look at everything in nature, and see the similarity, but when the individual object is studied the truth comes out that none are exactly the same. No two plants are identical, no two animals are exactly alike, no two rocks, and no two people are exactly the same. The bare moment of birth of identical twins makes one older than the other.

David in writing Psalm 8:4 and 5, considered the question of what man is? He writes, "What is man, that thou art mindful of him? and the son of man that thou visitest him? The answer to this question seems to evade all mankind, when it is simply stated in the Holy Bible. We are to be the children of God, and as such we are in training to become like God and like Christ. For this reason, God has shown favoritism in choice above all other creatures and has given man his blessing above all other creations.

In the physical form, we are a creation still in the making, and this is answered in Psalm 8:5, "For thou hast made him a little lower than the angels, and has crowned him with glory and honor. The glory and honor is having been created in the image and likeness of God, and will someday be the children of God. This has a further explanation.

The right to be a child of God is given freely to man by God, but man must make the choice to either follow God's instructions to immortality, or to follow man's own intellect and foolhardiness, and become allied with Satan, against God. These are the two choices each person has before them, and they must decide which to follow. The worthiness of each individual determines whether they will become a child of God, and become immortal, or if the individual is to be destroyed out of existence in the lake of fire. The choice rests with the individual.

There is in the world the idea held by many, that they will live life to the evil side, and just before the day of judgment jump to the other side and be saved. These disillusioned people have been deceived into a plan that won't work. You have to declare yourself, and it works like this. If you believe in God, but not Jesus Christ, as they do in the Islamic and Judaic religions, you will be judged on your works. Very few will be found worthy. Prior to Christ coming to earth, blood sacrifice of animals was used in conjunction with prayers to obtain mercy for sins, but with Christ giving his blood as the final blood sacrifice, the blood sacrifice no longer is recognized by God as atonement for sins. Many Christians have the false notion they can do anything and be pardoned by asking forgiveness in Christ's name, but that isn't the case. The act committed is evil, the asking for forgiveness must be based on behavior change, and in Christ's name, and the forgiveness comes sometime after your behavior has changed. It comes in the form of forgetting the evil ever happened. So it is that a simple little lie may be quickly forgotten, but the killing of another individual is never forgotten. The pain of having committed the sin is gone, but remembrance lingers to remind one and all not to trespass further.

Science is aware of the differences between man and beasts, but they are careful never to admit to them while pushing the atheist theory of evolution. It pays to read and heed what God has to say about man, and his two bodies. The one statement in the Holy Bible that destroys the theory of evolution is written in I Corinthians 15:38, "But God giveth it a body as it hath pleased him, and to every seed his own body. Evolution does play a small part in life, but nothing ever came into being because of "survival of the fittest dogma preached by science. Each and everything that is alive on the planet came from God's planning and decrees, and man was his greatest achievement. It's a simple format. God wanted a being that would be a replica of himself, and so he created man in his image and likeness. That means that man is the only being alive that has the capacity to be a living God outside of God himself. The difference between man and God is this. God is in three persons, the Father, the Son, and the Holy Ghost. Man is only of two bodies, mortal man, and spiritual man. We lack the perfection of the third.

How is man separated from the beasts of earth? The first difference is that we are created in the image and likeness of God, and that makes us unique. While animals also have physical life, they do not have a spiritual life, so that becomes a very large difference. Then there is the testimony given in I Corinthians 15:39, "All flesh is not the same flesh: but there is one kind of flesh of men, another flesh of beasts, another of fishes, and another of birds. Just about every one is aware of this difference, but science chooses to ignore this fact. Why they refuse to accept this difference is because it threatens the theory of evolution, and that man is nothing more than an animal. Despite their trying to prove otherwise, over the years science has had to admit there are four distinctive blood groups in man, and that these blood types have to be compatible if a blood transfusion is needed. For this reason the blood bank, and blood donor program has been set up to fill this need.

Animals have one type of blood, and it is interchangeable throughout species, but not with man. If man were an animal, then his blood would be the same as the beasts, and there would be no need for the blood donor program, because there would be an adequate supply from animals. Such isn't the case, so science is totally wrong in saying man is an animal.

The same is true with organs, skin, or any other part of the body. People have some of the same organs as animals, but there are differences that cannot be bridged by medical science. Even between people, the person receiving a transplant usually has to stay on anti rejection medication the rest of his life, otherwise the body would reject the transplanted organ. Common sense dictates that if transplants can be performed in beasts without rejection, but cannot be done in man without rejection, then it has to be reasoned that man is different from animals.

When God created Adam ftom the dust of the ground, and breathed into his nostrils the breath of life, he not only performed a function in CPR, but he imparted to Adam part of his own Spirit. This means all mankind has the Spirit of God residing in them, and this is the intent of I Corinthians 15:44, "It is sown a natural body; it is raised a spiritual body. There is a natural body, and there is a spiritual body.

During the time Adam walked and talked with God, they were in spiritual and physical communion with one another. Adam learned to let the spiritual body rule over his physical body and the reason why is written in I Corinthians 3:16, and 17, "Know ye not that ye are the temple of God, and that the Spirit of God dwelleth in you? If any man defile the temple of God, him shall God destroy; for the temple of God is holy, which temple ye are. It takes some effort to trust your body to the guidance of the spiritual body, but it has to be remembered the Spirit of God resides in the temple, and not the temple in the spirit. The Holy Ghost acts in concert with the Spirit of God residing in the physical body, and since the Holy Ghost, and the Spirit of God cannot make a mistake, they will lead the body down the road of righteousness, and immortality.

A lot has been said about the two bodies of man, and there need be an application of the principles to gain full understanding. Two social issues will be used to demonstrate how the principles apply in everyday life. The first social issue is that of abortion.

Science in its atheist teaching has declared that a fetus is nothing more than an unwanted piece of flesh in a woman's body, and should be removed at the woman's request, without question, and without penalty. The Supreme Court of the United States of America has declared it is lawful for a woman to undergo an abortion up to and including partial live birth, at which time the infant is destroyed and removed. Many believe this is very unethical but few, if any, can cite the reason why it is so damning to the woman, the doctor, and those involved in any such procedure, maybe even extending to the judge.

We return to Isaiah 43:7, "Even every one that is called by my name: for I have created him for my glory, I have formed him; yea, I have made him   God knows us by our name before we are ever born, and this is made clear in Jeremiah 1:5, "Before I formed thee in the belly I knew thee; and before thou camest out of the womb I sanctified thee, and I ordained thee a prophet unto the nations.

The concept that birth is decided by man and not God is the work of the Devil, and the Devil is at work convincing man that God doesn't know anything, and it's the same line he used in deceiving Eve to eat of the forbidden fruit. "Go ahead and eat of it, he tells Eve, "God knows that by eating it you'll be like him, and won't die. This line of reasoning is in use today by having impregnation done in a dish, then implanted into a woman, and farther out the newest idea, that of cloning people.

Since it is obvious God knows each person before they are ever conceived by woman, it should be obvious that God sent the individual to earth, and the reason he sent the person to earth was to accomplish a specific work. In reasoning it out, by destroying the fetus in the woman, the spirit assigned that body cannot complete the work God scheduled for doing. At the same time, despite the Supreme Court's ruling that a child has no rights until it is born live, in God's court these people will stand in judgment for having murdered one of God's people, and for having defiled God's temple, the physical body. These are serious sins, and are punishable by being destroyed out of existence. This destruction isn't physical death, but is the total destruction of the body and spirit in the lake of fire, making it as though that person had never existed in the first place.

Man has the inner trait of wanting immortality, and has the awareness of existing, and the fear of death. The fear of death is the result of not knowing for sure if life continues after death or not? An animal doesn't fear death because they have no conception of life or death. Their instinctive behavior allows them to survive, but they cannot worry because they have no formulated consensus of what is life, what is death. The explanation is this. The reasoning ability of an animal is severely limited. An animal's behavior can be altered by training, and sometimes by experience, but they cannot reason any more that it takes to survive. A bird coming to a feeder each day to check for seed is conditioned on the seed being there, and the bird may check for several days after the food source is removed, but thereafter it will check only occasionally, as it starts to rely on natural food sources.

The quest for immortality by man is well known in man's history, the search for the fountain of youth, a way to medically postpone old age, and the search for the magic herb that will lengthen life. Why else would medical science try to prolong the years of man, if it were not a search for immortality? Beasts age, and move away to die, even as a flower dies in the first freeze of autumn. To them death is just an occurrence, but to man it is either the beginning of a spiritual life, or the end of a physical life and oblivion, depending on what the person believes.

The far reaching judgment of God extends to those like the judges of the Supreme Court of the United States for their part in the murder of the unborn. If they are to render caustic judgment on the unborn, sent by God to earth, their judgment by God will be just as caustic or maybe more so. There is this to say about whether or not God has the right to effect judgment. It should be obvious that everything in existence had to come from God, because in the beginning, there was only God. That means everything in existence belongs to God, and if everything is his property, then he can do with it as he likes. Here's what God says in Isaiah 43:13, "Yea, before the day was I am he; and there is none that can deliver out of my hand: I will work and who shall let it?

Man has taken it upon himself to believe (like Satan) he can rival God, and that makes his ego a danger unto himself. God recognized this trend in man way back in the time of the tower of Babel. In Genesis 11:6 is recorded, "And the Lord said, Behold the people is one, and they have all one language; and this they begin to do: and now nothing will be restrained from them, which they have imagined to do. While most inventions were created for the betterment of man, most have been converted from practical and good use, to use as evil works.

The auto is a wonderful machine because it saves lives in the form of the ambulance, gives people the ability to travel long distances in short time, and gives a traveling home in the form of a recreational vehicle. Surely there can be no argument that the auto is a wonderful invention, until you look at the bleak side of the picture of them becoming a war machine, a conveyance for illicit drug travel, and as a murder weapon.

The same can be said of firearms, matches, knives, or any other invention. If it can be converted to evil use it will be done. This is exactly what has happened to doctors performing abortion, mercy killings, and euthanasia. They were given the knowledge to heal, but they have converted that skill to doing evil. It is doubtful that mankind will ever awaken to his errors, and bad behavior, and progress to the rightful status as being children of God, which is as near being a God, as is possible, without actually being God himself.

The second social issue to be examined is that of the homosexual relationship, and its place in society. The courts are slowly caving into the pressure of the homosexual men and women to make legal the behavior described by God as an abomination. The thinking of man has become so distorted that people have come to believe that when a sin is committed, it is against another person, and everyone need understand that all sin is a sin against God, and not man. Even the act of murder is an act against God, and not an act against fellow man, because the defiling of the temple (the physical body) houses the Spirit of God, so the act is perpetrated against the Spirit of God, and that makes it a sin. To slay a beast is not a sin, because though the life spirit is obliterated, the Spirit of God is not involved. This is why a beast can be slain without reproach, but the slaying of a man requires retribution by God.

The behavior of the homosexual is the defiling of the temple of God, the physical body, and God has deemed this abomination as being worthy of death. The first known instance of homosexual behavior on a large scale is recorded in chapter 19 of Genesis.

The emphasis by medical science is that homosexual behavior is a genetic problem, and that is to say that God turned out an imperfect product. The real cause of homosexual behavior is training. Homosexual behavior is a learned behavior, and is not instinctive, as science and homosexuals would have you believe. In the same vein of thinking, a drug addict can say his addiction is of genetic origin because some of his genes might be damaged. Whether the addiction is to behavior of using drugs, or to the behavior of having homosexual relations, the end result is behavior, not the product. Bestiality, having sexual intercourse with a beast, the raping of the young, the act of having intercourse with the dead, the raping of the old, and every other form of sexual deviation is behavior failure. The sexual predator rate is increasing as the world grows more secular in belief The same increase in homosexual relationships is occurring because of secular belief, and not because of genetic imbalance.

The scene in Genesis 19:4 proves beyond a doubt that a homosexual relationship is a learned behavior, and not a genetic, or instinctive behavior. Sodom and Gomorrah were two cities having homosexual populations, and God sent two angels down from heaven to destroy the cities. God is talking to Abraham about the cities, and Abraham asks God if he'd destroy the righteous with the evil? They bargain back and forth until it is decided, that if ten righteous persons could be found in the city of Sodom, then the city would be spared. In the city was Lot, his wife, and two daughters who were straight, so actually only six more straight people had to be found for the city to be saved.

The two angels arrive in Sodom, and Lot convinces them to stay at his house instead of spending the night in the street, because he knew how the men of Sodom were with strange men in town. The action is now centered on Genesis 19:4, "But before they lay down, the men of the city, even the men of Sodom, compassed the house round, both old and young, all the people from every quarter.

There were both old men and young men, and since Sodom was far away from other cities and towns, it is obvious these young men were born in Sodom, because people didn't have the means to travel like today. Most settled very close to where they were born. The population of Sodom had to be Homosexual men, lesbian women, and the bisexual who had sexual relationships with both men and women. The offspring from these relationships were raised in a city where homosexual behavior was the normal, and having been raised in that environment, the young took up the homosexual behavior.

Without finding ten straight or righteous people in the town, the angels told Lot to take his wife and daughters and leave the city, and not look back. The cities were then destroyed by fire and brimstone.

In Leviticus is the commandment of God concerning homosexual relationships. It is first written in Leviticus 18:22,

"Thou shalt not lie with mankind, as with womankind: it is abomination. Then in Leviticus 20:13, it is further defined, "If a man lieth with mankind, as he lieth with a woman, both of them have committed an abomination; they shall surely be put to death; their blood shall be upon them.

From somewhere came the notion that the laws of old time are no longer valid in today's world, but this is incorrect. Every law God has put out is as steadfast as the laws of physics. If there is a flaw it is because man was wrong in his first assessment, but the laws put out by God do not change except by his changing them. There is a reason for this, and it is that if God constantly changed the law, as man does, what could be construed as being right and just? Suppose for a moment that God said he was waiving murder as being a sin? Would killing other people increase or decrease? Isn't it the fear of incurring the wrath of God that stays the hand from committing such an atrocity? Surely the law administered by man, life imprisonment, or other such decrees do not fulfill God's law. Man is not authorized to pardon or forgive sin that is perpetrated against God, and in most cases the sin is against God, and not man. Families forgiving someone who has murdered one of the family members are in effect saying God is pardoning the murderer, and that simply isn't true. No man can speak for God in this present day, that is why we have the Holy Bible. We are to use that as our guide through life.

There is another point and it is what happens when a person does commit sin. From the time a sin is thought by a person, until the completion of the action, the Holy Ghost absents himself from the person, because this most Holy entity cannot abide evil, and after presenting his argument within the person, if the intent to sin is there, the Holy Ghost vacates the temple until the sin is committed. In some, so many sins are committed, or thought of being committed, that the Holy Ghost is mostly absent from the temple (the physical body of man) and that void is filled by Satan. The primary goal of Satan is to occupy God's throne, and part of that comes through enslaving God's people to evil rebellion against God, and the way he does this is by entering a person's body to occupy the temple, and in doing so, defiles the temple. The more defiled the temple becomes, the stronger the alliance with Satan becomes, because Satan's influence is dominant over man whenever sin is committed. It can be said that all sin is committed in Satan's name, and all goodness is committed in God's name.

In weighing out the truth, and in using the Holy Bible to reconcile what is the absolute truth, there becomes the factor of understanding the language and meaning of the Holy Bible. Most have given little thought to the subject, but the Holy Bible is written in common language of the day, and for this reason.

Language flows from the past to the present, but never present to the past. We are given to understand what the prophets said, but how many old time prophets could understand the language we use today? For that matter, how could a person today understand what the language will be say 5000 years ahead? Some key words may yet be in use, but for all practicability, the language will have changed dramatically. How many people of Christ's day would understand such words as "Roger willco and out ? Few today understand that it means I understand and will comply and it is the end of the radio transmission. The language today contains many abbreviated names, such as Inc., NAFTA, NYPD, NATO, SEATO, UPS, and a host of others that are common to people today, but would have completely baffled people a few years ago. A demonstration of how the language of the Holy Bible flows forward can be seen in this example.

In the olden time, the learned men of the day, who were the fore runners of today's modern scientists, believed the earth was flat, and a ship sailing too far out from shore would fall off the edge of the earth. This belief was widespread enough so that some cultures believed the earth rode on the back of a huge turtle, and in another culture it was believed the earth was supported by four giant elephants. A person has to wonder why they thought this way back then, and it was because at the time, they made some observations that led them to this conclusion. These same observations can be made today. When you stand on a plain of ground, or on a deck of a ship at sea, the horizon looks like a straight line, and the intervening land or water looks flat. This is because the curvature of the earth cannot be seen. Even from the top of the highest mountain on the planet, the height is not sufficient to see the curvature of earth. There is also the phenomena of when the sun or moon is seen, they appear as flat disks, because to the naked eye no discerning curvature can be seen. These observations led men to believe that earth, like the sun and the moon was a flat disk shaped object. Given what information they had, the theory was a reasonable conclusion.

It wasn't until Christopher Columbus set sail, and completed a voyage without falling off the earth's edge, that the round earth (globe shaped) theory came into being. For awhile the two theories were used, but gradually the flat earth theory became secondary to the round earth theory. Christopher Columbus set a new standard for travel, and today we sail the same seas in a few days, or zip across them aboard a jet liner in just a few hours. The round earth theory remained a theory until the first astronauts viewed earth from orbit in outer space, and televised pictures of the earth back to the people of earth, revealing that the earth was a round globe like structure. At that time, the flat earth theory was entirely discarded, and the round earth theory was proven factual. It is now accepted world wide that the earth is a round globe shaped planet.

Christopher Columbus has gone down in history as the man proving the earth round, and the astronauts are lauded as being the first men to see earth from outer space. The round earth theory has only been around 500 years, a rather short time in man's history, and that means for 6500 years man thought wrong about the earth. However it may be, Christopher Columbus wasn't the first man to know the earth was round, and the astronauts were not the first to view earth from outer space. The first man to achieve both of these distinctions was the man named Isaiah, and he lived 2500 years ago. We can read his account of the event in Isaiah 40:22, "It is he that sitteth upon the circle of the earth, and the inhabitants thereof are as grasshoppers; that stretcheth out the heavens as a curtain, and spreadeth them out as a tent to dwell in.

The first question that can be asked is, "How did Isaiah know the earth was a circle or round? It has already been declared that until the day when Christopher Columbus made his epic voyage, there was no way to determine the earth was round, because the curvature of the earth cannot be determined except from a very great height, and not even the tallest mountains in the world is sufficiently high for this purpose.

This means that Isaiah had to view the earth from somewhere above, and it had to be in outer space. This becomes more logical when the next part of the verse is examined, "... and the inhabitants thereof are as grasshoppers.... In what way is man like a grasshopper? Surely Isaiah wasn't comparing man's general physical appearance to the grasshopper, because there is virtually little likeness between the two. While it is true that hordes of grasshoppers swarmed over the earth at times blotting out the sun, Isaiah couldn't be comparing the population of man to that of grasshoppers, because man had not yet reached a great population. Most were nomads, wandering over the land in search of grazing for their animals, and living off the earth. The only other comparison that could be made is size, and this gives a clue to Isaiah's words. The only time man could be compared in size to a grasshopper is during the ascent to altitude. There are very few who have boarded an airplane, and not remarked about the effects after takeoff, as the person watched the land fall away from distinguishable fields to a patchwork of color, and buildings become scaled down versions like doll houses, and people become as small in appearance as ants. This is what Isaiah was trying to get across, but since ants were probably nonexistent where he lived, and grasshoppers were common, Isaiah used grasshoppers as a measurement. Fleas were present, but too small for people to relate to, but grasshopper was a familiar sight, and Isaiah used that as the model. His next view "...that stretcheth out the heavens as a curtain.... de notes another familiar thing to the people of that time. Curtains were common. The tents they used were made of panels of cloth or skins, and were called curtains. Curtains also were used to separate the tent into different rooms, so the term curtain means a sheet of some type. When Isaiah reached the altitude to view earth, he probably saw the spiral arm of the galaxy in which earth is located. In the summer we see this as a band of stars, and we call it the Milky Way, which is also the name of out Galaxy. Isaiah compares this sheet of stars as like a spread out curtain, and this statement is not much different from writers of today.

When a writer writes, "A canopy of stars was overhead, we know by his description that stars fill the night sky. Is it then much different to say. "a curtain of stars stretched out before me? It is in the understanding that common words, objects, and events were used by the prophets to illustrate similarity of heavenly sights and events, and understanding this gives clarity to the Holy Bible.

The last part of the verse is also descriptive of what Isaiah saw. "... and spreadeth them out as a tent to dwell in. When a person is in a tent, or even a room, they are aware there is a roof, four walls, and a floor. This encloses them in a shell, just as a peanut is enclosed in a shell. What Isaiah saw from his vantage point was that earth had stars all around it, enclosing it like a tent to dwell in, or like a peanut in a shell. This is a remarkable incident, one that people know today is absolutely correct in observation, which means Isaiah had to have made the journey. Because we know that man cannot live in the harsh environment of outer space without protective pressure clothing, and must have an atmosphere created in his suit, it is possible to say that Isaiah was probably lifted spiritually aloft by God to view earth, and to tell what he saw. This is not unlike the testimony of John, who was imprisoned on the isle of Patmos, but was lifted spiritually to heaven to record the book of Revelation.

The object of the example is to demonstrate that thinking and application is required in order to benefit from the wisdom and truth of the Holy Bible. It can also be noted that in the use of the Holy Bible, references from several different books in the Holy Bible are quoted, and this is what is pointed out in Isaiah 28: 10, "For precept must be upon precept, precept upon precept; line upon line, line upon line; here a little and there a little. A demonstration of this is given so each person can see how the verse of the Holy Bible supplement, and support every other verse, ethic, and idea of the Holy Bible.

We start in Proverbs 9: 10, "The fear of the Lord is the beginning of wisdom: and the knowledge of the holy is understanding. Why should we fear the Lord? Hasn't it been voiced that God is good, God is forgiving, God is tolerant, and God is love? If he is these things, then why should we fear him? The answer comes from Jesus, and it is written Matthew 10:28, "And fear not them which kill the body, but are not able to kill the soul: but rather fear him which is able to destroy both soul and body in hell. From what is said, man has a soul and a body, and this takes us right back to I Corinthians 15:44, "It is sown a natural body it is raised a spiritual body. There is a natural body and there is a spiritual body. This gives you the

31

thread of truth in one portion of the verse, but there is much more information in the verse.

There is a place called Hell, and there has been a lot of distortion of what hell is like. Hell is a place just as Heaven is a place, and Earth is a place. Hell is divided into two compartments, one called Hades, and one called Sheol. To most of us, Hell isn't where we want to go, but this is where there is misunderstanding about hell. Before visiting there, it has to be considered what happens when a person dies, and this first mentioned in Genesis 3:19, when God was angry with Adam, and he speaks these words, "In the sweat of thy face shalt thou eat bread, till thou return unto the ground; for out of it wast thou taken: for dust thou art, and unto dust shalt thou return. There isn't a way for the human body to become anything more than dust, and regardless of how we die, our flesh and bones will return someday to dust. What happens to the physical body is then clear, but if man has the Spirit of God as the Scriptures say, then what happens to that at the time of death? The answer to this question is answered in Ecclesiastes 12:7, "Then shall the dust return to the earth as it was: and the spirit shall return unto God who gave it. That's pretty clear as to what's going to happen, but there need be a little bit more known about the spirit dwelling within us, and this is explained quite fully in I Corinthians 2:12, 13, and 14, "Now we have received, not the spirit of the world, but the spirit which is of God; that we might know the things that are freely given to us by God. Which things also we speak, not in the words which man's wisdom teacheth, but which the Holy Ghost teacheth; comparing spiritual things with spiritual. But the natural man receiveth not the things of the Spirit of God: for they are foolishness unto him: neither can he know them, because they are spiritually discerned. This is the same as was presented earlier. The Spirit of God resides in each of us, and without the Spirit of God we would be like animals, given only to instinctive behavior.

Since we have the spirit of God dwelling in us, it can be noted, that when the physical body expires, the spirit is released from the temple, which is the physical body, and this is shown to be the case in recent well-documented incidents This fact has been experienced by people having what is called, a out of body experience, and the incidents have been carefully recorded and examined, and accepted as real happenings. It appears that a person is on their death bed due either to a serious accident, or an acute illness. The spiritual body rises to be above the physical body which is being worked on by doctors in an effort to revive the person. The spiritual body can hear every word spoken by the doctors, and this was taken into account in the evaluation of the stories. The spiritual body is drawn toward an aperture where a bright light beckons them. It is describes as being something like a light being shown from one end of a dark tunnel. The spiritual body is drawn toward the light, and at some point they are told they must return. They awaken to find that are starting to recover health in their physical body. Are these stories true? There is reason to believe they are, and this observation is based upon Biblical Scriptures. In Matthew 17: 1, is written the account where Jesus wanted to talk to Moses and Elias, and since they were physically dead, Jesus transfigured himself before Peter, James, and John and spoke with Moses and Elias. Why did he have to change to a spirit? It is forbidden for man to communicate with the dead, and we are given an example of this in I Samuel 28:7. Samuel was dead, and the Philistines were ready to attack the Jews under Saul. It was then Saul decided to try and talk to Samuel through a woman in Endor. In Samuel 28:7 is written, "Then said Saul unto his servants, Seek me a woman that hath a familiar spirit, that I may go to her, and enquire of her. The servants then take him to Endor. In exchange, Saul had to promise the woman that he would not have her killed, as the law dictated. In Samuel 28:12,13, and 14, is a description of what the woman saw, and then in verse 15 we read, "And Samuel said to Saul, Why have you disquieted me? The communication with the dead is forbidden by God, and those having a familiar spirit, namely wizards, and witches, mediums, magicians and the like are covered under Leviticus 20:27, "A man or woman that hath a familiar spirit, or that is a wizard, shall surely be put to death: they shall stone them with stone. Their blood shall be upon them. While it is that most mediums, fortune tellers, magicians, and the like are masters at deception, very skilled in using information a person relates to them first, there are some who have the power of a witch or wizard. This practice hasn't been eradicated from the world as yet, and the living proof seems to be in some of the voodoo religious rites that can cause death.

The conversion from physical to the spiritual is then what occurs when the physical body expires, and in Luke 16:19 through 26, the whole thing is explained. "There was a certain rich man, which was clothed in purple and fine linen, and fared sumptuously every day: And there was a beggar named Lazarus which was laid at his gate, full of sores, and desiring to be fed with the crumbs which fell from the rich man's table: moreover the dogs came and licked his sores. And it came to pass, that the beggar died, and was carried away by the angels into Abraham's bosom: the rich man died also and was buried. When the spirit leaves the body it goes either to Sheol or Hades, depending upon how life on earth was lived. Lazarus was carried by the angels to Sheol, into the bosom of Abraham.

The rich man woke up in Hades, the part of Hell where the unworthy are tortured. We continue on in Luke 16:23, "And in hell he lift up his eyes, being in torments, and seeth Abraham afar off, and Lazarus in his bosom. And he cried and said, Father Abraham. have mercy on me, and send Lazarus, that he may dip the tip of his finger in water, and cool my tongue; for I am tormented in this flame. But Abraham said, Son, remember that thou in thy life time receivest the good things, and likewise Lazarus evil things: but now he is comforted, and thou art tormented. And beside all this, between us and you there is a great gulf fixed: so that they which would pass from hence to you cannot: neither can they pass to us that would come from thence.

The thread of truth now expands to what extent does being rich have on what happens to a person after death. This rich man went to hell and was tormented in flame, while the poor beggar went to Abraham's bosom and was comforted. To get the answer to this, we have to go to Matthew 19:23 and 24, to read what Christ said about it. Matthew 19:23 and 24, "Then Jesus said unto his disciples, Verily I say unto you, that a rich man shall hardly enter into the kingdom of God. And again I say unto you, It is easier for a camel to go through the eye of a needle, than for a rich man to enter into the kingdom of God. Why, after hearing the words from Christ, does man insist on trying to own everything in the world? Why are we so dedicated to greed? What makes man desire more than he could ever possibly use ? Most of all, why do people have the false notion that when God promises prosperity, people believe he means wealth or richness? The answer is clear about being wealthy, and it is written in Matthew 6:19, 20, 21 and 24, "Lay not up for yourselves treasures upon earth, where moth and rust doth corrupt, and where thieves break through to steal: But lay up for yourselves treasures in heaven, where neither moth nor rust doth corrupt, and where thieves do not break through to steal: For where your treasure is, there will be your heart also. No man can serve two masters: for either he will hate the one, and love the other; or else he will hold to the one, and despise the other. Ye cannot serve God and mammon. Mammon is money.

It becomes obvious that as a person gains wealth, he runs toward the source of wealth and away from God, and that is the source of evil connected to money. If you, in your greed, seek after the riches of the world, you lose the wealth you stored in heaven. Christ is saying, lay up your treasure in heavenly things that your spirit will be rich in heavenly abundance, just as Lazarus lounged in comfort after his physical demise.

The use of the Scriptures have been demonstrated well enough for a person to follow through, and gain the absolute truth from the Scriptures. One needs no instruction to do this, the Holy Ghost will do the instructing as you read and contemplate the meaning of the different verses. It is only in this way a person can gain the knowledge God wants the person to have, but it must be a genuine effort, and the person must ask God in prayer to give him the knowledge he seeks. The atheist, and the agnostic can scream to high heaven, saying, how can you say such, when it has never been proven that a God exists? In fairness to their side of belief, we need ask, Does a God exist? This is where the two major factions disagree. The atheist says there is no God, and the religious say that a God does exist. Which is right? It can be reasoned out to a satisfactory conclusion in the following way.

When a person goes out of doors, they are aware there is a sun, and there is a moon. They know the sun is many times bigger than the earth, and that the moon is about one sixth the size of earth. From this observation it can be concluded that the Universe must be made up of different sized objects, and that means there has to be a biggest something, and there has to be the littlest something. To science, the leader in the atheist belief, the largest known object in existence are the super galaxies, which are clusters of galaxies. On the other end of the scale, the weakon, a sub atomic particle is the smallest known particle discovered so far.

The difference between the religious and the atheist is that according to what is said, the Universe itself is recognized by the religious as an object, whereas; the atheist dare not recognize the Universe as an object, because in doing so, it would be an admission there is something outside the Universe, and that would defeat the theory of evolution and the big bang theory.

Going back now to the sun, the moon, and the earth, we know that the sun is much more powerful than the earth, and the earth is at least six times more powerful than the moon, and from this observation we can conclude the Universe is made up of different levels of power. The scientists of today, say super galaxies are the greatest power so far discovered, and the weakon again is distinguished as the weakest power in the Universe so far discovered.

The religious contend there is a Highest power outside the Universe, and he created the Universe as an object. This power is recognized as the Highest power in existence and is referred to by the religious as a God. The point is this. Regardless of which way a person believes, there is a Highest power, and they are sorted out by the religious physically as the Creator God, and by the scientific community as an unknown force, waiting to be discovered. Many scientists believe the super galaxies are the most powerful force in the Universe, but then that discounts that the super galaxies are in orbit around the center of the Universe. This can be compared to saying earth is the strongest power in our solar system even though it orbits the sun.

It should be pretty obvious that science has to rethink its position on a lot of these theories, and they are currently doing just that, but most are totally stumped in the effort to come up with a new theory that retains the atheist belief, and supports the theory of evolution.

The answer of course lies in the fact that it has to be established that God does exist, and there has to be an explanation of how the Universe, earth, and man came into existence. This is to come shortly. For now it is enough to understand that from either side, a Highest power is recognized, and to the religious that Highest power is God, and to the atheist, it can be whatever they wish to call it.

It would seem proper that given the Holy Bible is the word of God, and the absolute truth, that it would be made central to everything on the planet, but that isn't the case at all. The Holy Bible holds the spotlight as being the world's all time best selling book, and along with that, it is the world's most wanted book. What is contrary about this is the fact that although more Holy Bibles are in circulation than any other book, it is not widely read. Though it is the most cherished of books, it is usually tucked away on a closet shelf, on the lower shelf of an end table, or between two books in a book shelf. Given its desirability a person would expect it to be displayed proudly in the home, office, or anywhere people were gathered. After all, God is God, and his word is the truth. Why then should it be tucked away from those he has given the word to? Is it because we are ashamed of believing in God? Have you ever noticed how few hymns are sung or hummed by people as they ride along in the car, walk along in the forest or meadow, or as they work on a tedious project? They have no qualms about singing, humming, or whistling a favorite modern song, but why not a song dedicated to God?

What makes people shy away from displaying their loyalty and devotion to God? This doesn't have to be a fanfare type thing. If a Christian, a cross can be worn, and in doing so, indicate the person is dedicated to God through Christ.

With the Holy Bible, it should be made central to the home, and the adult male, the father or eldest son, should make sure the family shares some of the word of God daily, by reading a verse or two from the book. By having a central place in the home, each member of the household is afforded the opportunity to consult the book openly, without any guiltiness associated with being religious and holy. Can it not be understood by all that man is a holy vessel having as the temple of God the physical body, and that the Spirit of God dwells within each person? Are we not then made holy by God's presence? The world of man has been plagued by the illogical, senseless, and violence of hearing, seeing, and learning the unholy, and it is time that man return to God's word, God's ethics, laws, and doctrine. Only then will some semblance of peace, tranquillity, and prosperity come about on earth. Unfortunately, that is not to occur until the return of Christ. The best the individual can hope to achieve is his own personal behavior and dedication to God.

Here are the closing words about the truth. It is written in Joshua 24:14, "Now therefore fear the Lord, and serve him in sincerity and in truth: and put away the gods which your fathers served on the other side of the flood, and in Egypt; and serve ye the Lord.

CHAPTER 2

Alpha and Omega

Does God exist? Is the Universe, earth and man his creations, or did they come about as science explains it in their theoretical models? How can there be anything certain discerned from the mass of information we've been bombarded with concerning the Universe, earth and man?

We need to first ask, Who is God, where did he come from, and what is he? Those sound like pretty tough questions, and they are for those who aren't interested in reading the truth in the Holy Bible, but for those willing to take the time to learn, they will lean all that is written here, and more beside.

Who does God say he is? There are many references to who God is, but he sums it up in Revelation 22:13, "I am Alpha and Omega, the beginning and the end, the first and the last. When this verse is read for the first time, it seems God is saying the same thing three different ways, and that's a valid understanding, but there is much more.

Alpha is the first letter of the Greek alphabet, and being the first letter it is also the beginning of the Greek alphabet. From this observation it can be said that Alpha, first, and beginning, are all the same. The same is true with the relationship of Omega, the end, and last. Omega is the last letter of the Greek alphabet, and being the last it is also the end of the Greek alphabet, and this establishes Omega, end, and last as being the same or synonymous in meaning.

There is another way to express the Alpha and Omega, the beginning and end, and first and last, and it is by use of the circle. The point where you begin to draw a circle is the very same point where you complete the circle. If it isn't you have drawn an arc, but not a circle. From this understanding the point of the beginning is the same point as the ending, and this can be expressed in comparison to God by saying that everything came from God, and everything must return to God. This establishes that God is the very beginning, and now it has to be determined where God came from. The answer to this question is found in Isaiah 43: 10, "Ye are my witnesses, saith the Lord, and my servant whom I have chosen: that ye may know and believe me, and understand that I am he: before me there was no God formed, neither shall there be after me.

The key word in this passage is the word "formed. God uses the word formed to indicate he has taken more than one element to make another element. To make sure this is the right track to follow, we look at Isaiah 45:7, "I form the light, and create darkness....

Science knows that visible light, the light we see from the sun, a light bulb, or a candle is made up of component lights. When visible light is put through a prism, it breaks down into the component lights, but God has gone one better than that. He has give us the rainbow which is visible light displayed in the different colors that make it up.

From this understanding, the word formed means that more than one element is used to make something else. However, when God uses the word create, it means to bring forth something never in existence before, and this is expressed in the verse by his saying, he creates darkness. While science knows quite a bit about light, they know absolutely nothing about darkness. Light has light rays or waves, but does darkness have rays? Does it have either of these qualities? Science doesn't know, and there is no definition of darkness as there is of light. Try to think of what darkness is? We see a shadow of blackness on the ground and we say it is because the source of light has been shut off, but what is that blackness? No one knows, and it's doubtful we'll ever know. For the purpose of this discussion, it will be used as a medium, in the same manner as light will be used as a medium.

Since God is a formed God, he is formed of more than one entity, and we know these three entities as God the Father, God the Son, and God the Holy Ghost. This is verified by John 1: 1, "In the beginning was the Word, and the Word was with God, and the Word was God. If the Word is with God, and the Word is God, we have to be reading about two separate entities joined together to be one. There are the three entities, and they form God. We know them from what their different duties are in the realm. God the Father is the Creator, and the overall boss outside the combined personage called God. God the Son is the Inheritor of the kingdom, and the Savior of man. God the Holy Ghost is the Instructor of man, and the Comforter of man. He is the Holiest part of the trio forming the merged entity known as God. For that reason, there is a stern warning about using blasphemy toward the Holy Ghost, and in this there is this to consider. If you curse God you are cursing the Holy Ghost because he is God, so it is better to refrain from all cursing. We find the warning in Matthew 12:31 and 32, "Wherefore I say unto you, All manner of sin and blasphemy shall be forgiven unto men: but the blasphemy against the Holy Ghost shall not be forgiven unto men. And whosoever speaketh a word against the Son of man, it shall be forgiven him: but whosoever speaketh against the Holy Ghost, it shall not be forgiven him, neither in this world, neither in the world to come.

We aren't privileged to know how the three entities came into existence, and perhaps they are some type of energy, and this is thought because upon the merging of the three entities that formed the single entity we know as God, at the joining, a bright light, many times brighter than our sun's light streaked out from the newly formed God. The distance outward the light reached is known to us as *Infinity*, distance without end, and the time it took for the light to cross this distance is called *Forever*, time without end. These two maximums are the boundaries or limits of God's power, and influence. Another term that is associated with these boundaries is the combination of infinity, distance without end, and forever, time without end. When these are combined it is called *Eternity*, distance and time without end.

What has to be shown is proof that this is the scene at the beginning, and that God is a source of light, and this is done in Revelation 22:5, "And there shall be no night there; and they need no candle, neither the light of the sun; for the Lord God giveth them light: and they shall reign forever and ever.

At the time the light streaked out to infinity and forever to establish the boundaries, it also established reality. There isn't any way to believe in something greater than infinity or for ever. Man simply can't conceive anything greater than that, and that means the limit of man's reality is infinity and forever. By the light radiating out from God in every direction, the same as the sun radiates light out in every direction, and traveling to infinity and forever a sphere of light was created in the two boundaries. This sphere of light is called Heaven, and it is where God is located. For the purpose of identification this Universe will be called the light Universe, and in this light Universe there is no time because time is defined as a period of darkness followed by a period of light. Since there is no darkness, there is no division, and though time does pass, it would not be recognized, so it can be said that in Heaven, the light Universe, there is no time, and therefore everything is immortal.

When it is said that time passes, but is not recognized, it can be compared to the time you are asleep. Time passes, but you are unaware of its passage until you wake up, and consult some reference to see how long you slept. The time passed, but without a measuring device, you wouldn't know what period of time passed.

Heaven, the light Universe, is established by God's light reaching out to the two boundaries, infinity and forever. At the same time, two very natural and basic laws come into existence, and they are the law of descending order, and the law of life spans. The law of descending order is this: Anything that is to be created has to be less than infinity and forever. This makes clear, that when God lays out the measurement of the physical Universe, which will be called the dark Universe, it must be less than infinity and forever. Since it is less than infinity and forever, it has a life span, and that is the second law. Anything that is to be created, must be less than infinity and forever and therefore will have a life span. These two basic laws are in effect, and we see them very clearly throughout all creation. Outside of heaven, the light Universe, the dark Universe we know as the Universe is largest known object. Since it is less than infinity and forever it is the oldest known object, and does have a limit to its life. Next in line, as far as science knows, are the super galaxies, and they may have a life span that might number in the billions of earth years. Then there are the galaxies, the solar systems, the planets, the moons, and on down into the subatomic region where the smallest of particles live. While the Universe itself may have a life span numbering in billions of years, the weakon's life span is measured in billionths of a second.

Science once thought the atom was the smallest known object, but again that theory has given away to the truth, and while the weakon is the latest discovery of smallest particles, science now believes the descending order goes on forever. That theory is in full accord with the mathematical truth, that if something is divided, there always remains something to divide.

With the boundaries of infinity and forever in place, and with the two laws the descending order, and the law of life spans in place, God is ready to bring forth the dark or physical

Universe. To find out how he did this we read Isaiah 50:3, "1 clothe the heavens with blackness, and I make sack cloth their covering. It should be noted that the darkness we see in the Universe is a covering which God likens to sackcloth, and it is important to remember that at some time God is going to remove that covering of darkness and make the physical Universe the same as the light Universe.

To picture what God did is to imagine a sphere of light that is the heaven or light Universe, and centered within this light Universe God put a sphere of darkness, which is to be the physical or dark Universe. God made the sphere of darkness for one purpose, so that when light was introduced into the darkness, the element of time would be created.

We are now at the stage of development where everything is in readiness for God to start having the angels assemble the different objects in the physical Universe. We leave this model of the beginning of the Universe to take a look at the model science theorizes as the beginning of the Universe.

Science claims that by looking through their giant telescopes, and other instruments they have looked at the faintest objects in the Universe and have concluded these faintest objects are also the most distant objects. What they are saying in effect is that by looking at the dimmest objects, they are concluding that these objects lie on the outermost part of the Universe, and are the oldest objects in the Universe. How they have come to reason this out is by using the speed of light as a constant. Science uses the speed of light, traveling at 186,200 miles per second, as a measuring device for the vast distances encountered in space. This is proven by the fact that earth is about ninety three million miles from the sun, and it takes about 8 or 9 minutes for the sun light to reach earth. From this it is reasoned the sunlight you feel is already eight or nine minutes old when it touches you. Given this fact, it can be concluded that light shining out from an object such as a star, would travel a specified distance in one earth year, and scientists call that distance one light year. Using this measurement, they have determined that the Milky Way galaxy, the one earth is located in, is 20,000 light years across, and 10,000 light years in depth. From this observation, when they look through space at the dimmest objects they believe they are looking back in time, or at the oldest objects in space. By using this thinking, they say they have looked back in time to a time called Planck time, which is the fraction of a second after the start of a gigantic explosion, called the big bang, which brought the Universe into being. This is based on two observations made by science. The first is the observation that every part of the Universe is moving away from every other part, and this simply means the Universe is expanding, or moving outward from a center. The second observation is that there is three degrees of radiation above absolute zero which pervades all space, and this radiation is theorized to be the after glow of the big bang.

Planck time is the fraction of a second after the start of the big bang, and the time when science says the laws of physics came into being. Planck time is a decimal point, forty two zeros and a one. It is a tenth of a thousandth, of a millionth, of a billionth of a trillionth of a trillionth of a second. This summary of the scientific model is roughly what science bases all their hopes on, but there are many unanswered questions, and they need be looked at.

"What existed before the big bang? The answer to this is that prior to the big bang every thing known or unknown, seen or unseen was compressed into an area smaller than an atom. So tightly compressed was this material that a teaspoon full would weigh billions of tons. The question then arises, if gravity, the compression force, wasn't available until after the start of the big bang, how could there be this super small super dense particle? This disparity cannot be answered by science, because if gravity didn't come out of the big bang, something had to create it before hand, and this destroys the theory. In answer, science says that technology hasn't yet reached a state to determine that.

"Where did the particle come from? The answer from science is that technology hasn't advanced far enough to make this determination.

"What caused the explosion? This is important because the laws of physics state a body at rest remains at rest until acted upon by a outside force. If the particle was at rest, and there's little reason to suppose it wasn't, then what caused it to activate to an explosion? To this question is the same answer, that technology to determine this isn't yet available.

It should be pretty obvious that the big bang theory has too many unanswered questions, and it's only fair to pose these same questions to the creation model. The creation model has God at the center, where his light radiates outward to infinity and forever, and the two laws, the law of descending order, and the law of life spans is in place. God then introduces a sphere of blackness in the center of the light Universe, and this darkness covers that portion of God's light. This is like having a bubble within a bubble, only the outer bubble is light, and the inner bubble is black. It can be see from this model that the physical Universe is then separated from the light or heaven Universe by the blackness. This separation is called by man, the spiritual Universe, where God dwells, and the physical Universe, where man dwells.

It is into this darkness that God is ready to lay out the objects in the Universe, and we read of it in Isaiah 48:13, "Mine hand also hath laid the foundation of the earth, and my right hand hath spanned the heavens: when I call unto them, they stand up together. From the verse it can be seen that the foundation of the earth was laid at the time God measured out the heavens. What was the foundation of the earth? This was the time the dark nebula that would become the Milky Way galaxy was formed. It is nothing but dust particles.

There is no reason to believe that heaven is any less physical than the physical Universe, but the heaven, or light Universe is in a different dimension than is the Universe we know. The proof is this. A number of years ago science figured out how much matter had to be in the Universe for it to act the way it does, but when they weighed out every source of matter in the Universe, they were way short of what was needed. This launched a search for the missing matter, and in the 1950's it was found in what science calls shadow matter. Shadow matter isn't anti matter. When anti matter and ordinary matter meet, they destroy one another. Shadow matter passes through ordinary matter without any reaction. Billions of shadow matter particles have just passed through the page you are now reading. Science has made the discovery that a parallel Universe is outside the physical Universe, and in the shadow matter Universe there may be as many as twelve different dimensions, instead of the three we have here, plus the time element. This discovery pretty well confirms that our Universe is only part of another Universe, and the Shadow matter Universe must be the light, or heaven Universe. It makes sense that with the cover of darkness, the particles making up the heaven Universe would still be present in this Universe, and the shadow matter seems to indicate that.

Science places the age of the Universe at 15 to 20 billion years old, and the earth about 4.6 billion years old. This again is saying by science that the light from the faintest, and most distant object took fifteen to twenty billion years to reach earth. This could be true if certain recent facts hadn't come to light. Three things have occurred that puts this theory to question.

The first is that science has found that light at the edge of the Universe is curved. This destroys the theory that light travels a specified 186,200 miles per second. Just as the air over the curved part of a wing goes faster than the air under the wing moving in a straight line, curved light has to travel faster than straight line light, because it covers more distance. Then too, the light speed of a laser has to be adjusted for temperature and humidity when used in land measurement, which again says that light speed is variable.

The second discovery was made in a laboratory, where scientists have accelerated light to a speed above the 186,200 miles per second, and this is a significant discovery. It had always been believed that the speed of light was a limit, and could never be exceeded, and it was believed that if the speed of light were to be reached, time as we know it would stop. By this experiment, these two more or less laws about light, are now proven untrue.

The third discovery about light was also a laboratory experiment in which light was slowed down to a mere 36 miles per hour. A later experiment by scientists has managed to stop light to zero miles per hour, and this literally destroys all earlier thinking and laws about light and its properties. What is most relevant is this. Anything that can be done in the laboratory can be done in the natural setting of the Universe. What this means is that light is variable throughout the Universe, and not confined to a single speed at any given moment. An example of this is that the light upon encountering a black hole, which is some kind of vortex or whirlpool, has to assume a curved course, and in doing so is accelerated faster and faster as it is drawn into a tighter circle within the whirlpool. Science knows this from observing stars disappearing into a black hole. This is demonstrated on earth by the created whirlpool in the sink. Objects on the outer reaches of the sink move slowly, but as they near the whirlpool of the drain, they are speeded up, and finally sucked down into the drain.

Without the light speed constant, all measurements of time and distance made by science are in error. A practical application is this. A boat is on the water doing eight knots, and there is a quartering wind of three knots. How long will it take for the boat to reach shore? Obviously, more information has to be obtained before the question can be answered. The starting point, and the ending point must be established before a time can be derived at, and then the variable of the wind must also be figured. Take this same example and apply it to a beam of light. The sun's light is radiated out into the galaxy and the space beyond, but how long will it take our sun's light to reach the limit of the Universe? First there must be some definitive distance to travel, and then the variables of objects that might deflect or alter the light's speed, such as a black hole, another galaxy or any unknown or undiscovered power, has to be figured in.

With this understanding it can be seen there is no way to estimate the age of anything by using light as the common measuring device. This is true about age of the Universe using the speed of light as a constant. >From the Bible it can be ascertained that the foundation of the earth, a dark nebula, was being created at the same time as God was measuring out the Universe. The word spanned, as used when he says, "... and my right hand hath spanned the heavens... means to measure using the distance between the thumb and little finger with the palm open.

The fact that God says he measured out the heavens means he had fore thought and planning, and this destroys science's notion that the Universe came into existence as a happenstance event. It is much more logical to believe that God planned out everything first, and then executed the plan, than to believe that on a whim, a microscopic particle erupted unto a gigantic explosion, and from this free explosion came the Universe and all it's objects.

Just about everyone has seen the burst of fireworks, where an explosion causes streaks of burning material to be thrown outward in the shape of a ball. If the big bang occurred, wouldn't it be more like the shrapnel of an exploding bomb or shell where no two pieces are the same? The fireworks display is a carefully manufactured product designed to operate one way, and it does so with precision, and the Universe also has these same attributes. In a bomb, or a shell burst, the pressure inside the hull of metal is uneven, and the shell hull gives way at the weakest points. These are random breaks, similar to how science believes the big bang occurred. How then can it be reasoned that the different objects in the Universe are symmetrical, that is, galaxies are galaxies, and stars are stars, and they are in order according to the law of descending order? Given the scientific model, how can objects be of different ages? If a burst brought into existence, everything that is in the Universe, then every bit and piece would have to be the same age, because they came from the same original source. One bomb or shell fragment is the same age as the other fragments, and there is no practical way to believe other than this. If the Universe then was from such an explosion, then the same rule would apply. Each piece of the Universe would be as old as any other piece, and this is another dilemma to science's model.

God now has the sphere of blackness and has measured out the Universe in readiness for the angels to bring together the elements that will create the different objects found in the Universe. The dust of the dark nebula, in which earth is to be born, is made, and the laws of physics are created. Now the angels work to put the objects into their correct position, and God tells us in Isaiah 48:13, in the last part of the verse, "...when I call unto them, they all stand up together. This indicates the objects, or at least the patterns of the objects of the Universe are established, and that the laws of physics is going to take over the completion of the creation. What is it that God says, that animates the whole system? We find it in Genesis 1:3, "And God said, Let there be light, and there was light.

The two observations made by science, and cannot be discounted, is the radiation of three degrees above absolute zero in all outer space. Absolute zero is defined as the temperature where molecular action ceases, and is around -400 degrees Fahrenheit. The three degrees above this point, means that molecular action is occurring, and this makes sense because if it were at the -400 degrees Fahrenheit nothing in the Universe could operate. How did this radiation come about? When God said, "Let there be light. all sources of light objects in a specific state of readiness burst into life, and since each object was closer into the center of the Universe, this sudden, but controlled event would approximate the theorized big bang of the scientific model. Here is the difference. In the cylinder of your car, the gas and air mixture is ignited by the spark plug, and moves across the top of the piston at a designated speed. This is a controlled burn, designed to give the maximum pressure at the correct time. Sometimes, when climbing a grade, or accelerating, a pinging sound comes from the engine, and that pinging sound is the gas and air mixture in the cylinder exploding instead of burning at a controlled speed. The result is the loss of power, and possible engine damage if the exposure lasts too long. The main point is that in one case the flame front is controlled burning, and in detonation it is a sudden explosion. The end result if we were looking at it, would be nearly identical sequences, but one is controlled, the other is not. When God set off all the different light emitting objects in the Universe, which were ready to ignite, that sudden ignition was very much like the spark plug and fuel air mixture in the cylinder burning at a controlled rate. This still would approximate science's big bang, and satisfactorily explains the three degrees of radiation.

At the time God started light through out the Universe, the whole Universe began to orbit about the center , and we see this in the galaxies, we see it in the solar system, and we see it in the atom. This pattern is a set pattern, and could not have come into existence without there being some type of plan and laws to guide it to this conclusion.

As the Universe began to orbit the center, centrifugal force began countering gravity. Gravity is the force that tries to compress everything into a single unit, and centrifugal force is the force that try to throw objects outward. These two forces were already created at the time God brought light into the Universe. The difference in heat in the Universe set it to rotating, and from this came the centrifugal force that tries to throw the objects outward from the center. From this it can be reasoned that centrifugal force at present is higher than gravity because the Universe is moving outward from the center, or expanding. This is in agreement with the scientific observation that the Universe is expanding, but since everything we know of in the Universe is subject to these two forces, it is easier to accept that centrifugal force is the reason it is expanding, than it is to believe the momentum was achieved by an explosion.

A look at how the two forces work is described very well where the mass of our galaxy, and the spiral arms of our galaxy orbit the center, and this is proven by the swept back arms of the galaxy. Our galaxy orbits a super galaxy which as far as we know, orbits the center of the Universe.

There is also this to consider. In having the dark, or physical Universe in the center of the light or heaven Universe, but in a different dimension, God has the best vantage point for overseeing his creation. And to us it is that heaven is always upward. By God's light radiating out from the center in the heaven or light Universe, and then having the bubble of darkness, of the dark or physical Universe also around the center, makes God the center of both the physical and heavenly Universe. This means God is the Highest power in the physical Universe we call home, and he is also the Highest power in the spiritual, or heaven Universe, which man also calls home.

There can be the understanding that God is then omnipresent in both Universes, because he is in each Universe at the same time, and this possible because the physical or dark Universe is located in the heavenly or light Universe.

For a great many years, science had the law of matter that said; matter could neither be created, nor destroyed. That law went up in the smoke of the atomic explosion. Since then, science has come up with the theory that matter came from light. It then becomes clear that since God is a source of light, as indicated in Revelation 22:5, then it follows the matter of the Universes, both the heaven or light Universe, and the dark or physical Universe came from God's light. This puts to an end the question of where the original matter of the Universe came from, and it surely goes a long way toward substantiating that everything came from God and everything has to return to God. This idea then agrees with what was said in the beginning, that God is Alpha and Omega, the beginning and end. It is the only logical conclusion that can be made in viewing all the facts and evidence from both a scientific and religious view point.

With the establishment of God as the Highest power in existence, there is more we should know about him, and how his truth fits into the overall picture. In being the Highest power in existence, anything God says is automatically made the truth, and this is because there is no power above him to contradict his word. This means that God cannot lie, because everything he utters becomes the truth. From this it can be said that God is Truth, and everything that was created was created in truth.

Look at another variation. Suppose for a moment that God could lie, and told a little white lie. What could be believed? Wouldn't his entire kingdom go to pieces because of disbelief?

The understanding that God cannot lie does wonders for man. It establishes the root belief that the word of God is truth, and that means the Holy Bible, on being God's word is the absolute truth. In the long run, if you go by what is said in the

Holy Bible, if you believe what is written in the Holy Bible, and if you practice the ethics in the Holy Bible, you are sure to be blessed by God, for God lives in truth.

In applying the truth that God is Alpha and Omega and what is written in the Holy Bible, it has been established that God, as Alpha was the very beginning. When he spoke the words which animated the whole physical Universe he introduced time, and time based on the scientific theory of the speed of light is proven unreliable. There is some consternation by people when they come to science's theory that it took the Universe to evolve for 15 to 20 billion years before man was born upon earth, and they are worried further when science says that earth is 4.6 billion years old. Why did God wait so long to bring forth man? Since science's theory is based on the speed of light, and proven wrong, what evidence is there of how things were done? For the answer to this we go to Isaiah 48:3, "1 have declared the former things from the beginning; and they went forth out of my mouth, and I shewed them; I did them suddenly, and they came to pass.

Time is defined as a period of darkness followed by a period of light. In the light Universe, where God's light is ever present, there is no time, and when the physical Universe was only a sphere of blackness, inside that blackness there is no time, because there is no light. Time began when the first streaks of light penetrated the darkness when God animated the physical Universe. That was the beginning of Universal time. Prior to that moment, even though time passed, nothing was aware of it because there was nothing to measure it against. In the beginning, the objects of the physical Universe were much closer together than they are now, and light passed between them more quickly than it does now. But that leads to the question are all the objects in the Universe moving outward at the same speed, or are those closer in moving outward slower than are those on the outer limits of the Universe? All these variables have to be taken into account if light is to be used as a measuring device. It is only when we apply the truth that time means a period of darkness followed by a period of light, that understanding can come. We get a clue to what God means when we read II Peter 3:8, "But, beloved, be not ignorant of this one thing, that one day is with the Lord as a thousand years, and a thousand yeas as one day. This is not a formula, but a statement that to God, a day might mean a thousand years, and used in this form, it can be reasoned as; "The day of the Lord. Each day is the Lord's day, but specifically it means the day that Christ is going to return to earth. In another use there are the six days of creation of earth that represents not earth days, but periods of time to getting specific periods of the creation accomplished. When God says he did something suddenly, we think of something going "poof and it appears, but when the creation period of the Universe is analyzed, it took time (which didn't count) for the angels to get everything ready according to God's plans, and then in a magic moment God said, "Let there be light. and everything went "poof and began working with clock like precision. So the word suddenly is like using the word wind, it has many different connotations. It might be a breeze, a gale, a hurricane, or several other descriptions, and when God uses words to express a time element like suddenly, it may mean in one instance, "poof right now, or it may mean similarly to when we say to a child, "Come here right now. We kn ow the child couldn't respond like "poof and be there, so there is a time interval we allow for his compliance. The best way to look at time in the Holy Bible is to carefully follow the events as they unfold. The birth of Christ was forecast 500 years before he ever arrived on earth, so time is relative only to what God wants to achieve at a specific time. Here's a problem for science to solve.

After Jesus was crucified and put in the tomb, on the first day of the week, Sunday morning, Mary was at the tomb, and dismayed because the tomb was empty. Then in John 20:17 is recorded, "Jesus saith unto her, Touch me not; for I am not yet ascended to my Father: but go to my brethren, and say unto them, I ascend unto my Father and your Father, and unto my God, and your God. That evening he appeared to the disciples, but Thomas wasn't among them. When the disciples told Thomas about Christ being there, he remarked that if he couldn't see the print of the nails in Christ's hands, and put his hand into the wound in Christ's side, he wouldn't believe that Christ had risen ftom. the dead.

Eight days later Jesus came again to the disciples, and he told Thomas to feel the imprint of the nails in his hands, and to thrust his hand into the wound in his side and believe. Because when Christ appeared to Mary, she could not touch him because he hadn't yet ascended to God, but he returned in eight days, and allowed Thomas to touch him. If as science says, the speed of light is the limiting thing in the Universe, and if God is located at the center of the Universe, How could Christ accomplish such a feat in eight days, when it takes twenty thousand light years just to cross our galaxy?

It can only be explained by realizing that when Christ ascended he went into the heaven Universe, from the physical Universe, and in the heaven universe there isn't any speed limit, and this leads to the idea there must be some type of portal between the heaven Universe and the physical Universe. Could that portal be the black holes we know exist in the physical Universe?

Science believes that if you went down into a black hole, you would emerge into another dimension and time. The idea of the portal explains why God can dispatch angels to do miracles on earth, and have them accomplished. Think about how many thousands or millions of years ago an angel would have had to been dispatched to do a miracle today, if as science says, the speed of light is a limit?

By there being portals between the heaven Universe and the physical Universe, angels could come and go as needed, and would be unhindered by speed in the heaven Universe. According to science the parallel Universe has up to twelve dimensions, and it stands to reason this parallel Universe is the heaven Universe or light Universe, and is in a different dimension from which we are in, and if angels are to cross over, there would have to be a portal, where they can change from spiritual to flesh, and revert back when they return to heaven. This is the only logical answer as to why miracles can and do happen, and removes the mystery of why angels appear and disappear from earth. It may also answer the question of why some people have absolutely disappeared from earth without ever being found or their remains discovered, and these missing people are the ones which people believe were kidnapped and taken aboard UFO's. It may also explain places like the Bermuda triangle, and the loss of people there without trace of them.

In there being a portal also explains why the physical body is left behind on earth, and the spiritual body goes to the heaven Universe. The heaven Universe being in a different dimension would require some type of transition, and it is done by the spirit going through the portal and not the physical body. In the heaven Universe, the person would appear the same as on earth in the physical form, but in a different dimension. This is seen in Revelation 1: 14, where it is written, "His head and his hairs were white like wool, as white as snow; and his eyes were as a flame of fire. This is the description of Christ in Heaven, but on earth he was a man of thirty-three years.

The Universe was created, and it was created according to what is written in Isaiah 45:18, "For thus saith the Lord that created the heavens; God himself that formed the earth and made it; he hath established it not in vain, he formed it to be inhabited. I am the Lord: and there is none else.

What's going to happen to the physical Universe we live in? If it is to have a life span, it must at some time expire. Since the Universe is less than infinity and forever, it has a life span, and that does lead to the conclusion there must come an end time. The prophets in the Holy Bible talk about the end time, Christ gave the signs to look for that will precede the end time, and the book of Revelation records what is to be in the end time, so it isn't as if we haven't been warned. And yet, despite this testimony, man continues to declare it will be, "World without end. and saying, "The ages will pass and change, but earth will endure.

Science says in its model that the Universe is expanding today, but at some time it will cease its outward movement, and begin to collapse back in toward the center, compressing back into the super dense, super small particle. This pretty much agrees with what is written in II Peter 3: 10, "But the day of the Lord shall come as a thief in the night; in the which the heavens shall pass away with a great noise, and the elements shall melt with fervent heat, the earth also, and the works that are therein shall be burned up.

Gravity is the compression force, and at present centrifugal force still has the Universe moving outward from the center, but there are indications that may indicate a change in this. The primary evidence is that science has viewed two galaxies passing through each other in opposite directions, and that has to mean that at least one galaxy has reached the boundary of the Universe and is on its way back toward the center. This verifies pretty well the scientific theory that when the objects reach the boundary of the Universe, they will rebound like a ball thrown against a wall.

The second bit of information is that science says that our star, the sun, will someday run out of the fuel it is now burning, and begin to burn the inner fuel, and this will cause it to expand into what they call a giant red star. In this expansion, the inner planets, Mercury, Venus, Earth, and Mars will be burned up. This seems to agree with what is written in Isaiah 30:26, "Moreover the light of the moon shall be as the light of the sun, and the light of the sun shall be sevenfold, as the light of seven days, in the day that the Lord bindeth up the breach of his people, and healeth the stroke of their wound. Up to recent times, science wasn't too concerned about the sun because they figured the sun was a middle aged star, with billions of years left to burn, but in the past year they have found the sun is heating up, actually getting hotter, and this is a concern.

If what is said is true, about the galaxies passing through one another, and the sun heating up, it seems to indicate that gravity is increasing throughout the Universe, and if so, it has to be because centrifugal force is decreasing. This means a slowing down of the Universe in its orbital path around the center. This does a couple of things. It dashes the hopes of those who believe that man might journey to another planet to escape the death of earth, and it should awaken man to the truth that an end time is coming.

In considering the expansion of the Universe, Isaiah 45:12, gives a good description of it, "I have made the earth, and created man upon it: I even my hands, have stretched out the heavens, and all their host have I commanded. Stretched is an outward motion, and commanded means in an orderly fashion. This means the objects in the Universe are moving outward in an orderly fashion, and this agrees with science. The only real hope that man has is what is written of the end time in Isaiah 51:6, "Lift up your eyes to the heavens, and look upon the earth beneath: for the heavens shall vanish away like smoke, and the earth will wax old like a garment, and they that dwell therein shall die in a like manner: but my salvation shall be for ever, and my righteousness shall not be abolished.

From the evidence, both scientific and Biblical, it should be apparent there is going to come an end time, and while there is no sure way to guess when the end will come, it is better to be prepared than not. The signs in the heavens and on earth seem to indicate that we are standing at the threshold of the end time, and are about to cross over into the time when things in the Universe, and on earth begin to become obvious we are in the end time. Unfortunately, those who have not committed themselves to God and Christ are going to find themselves in a pickle so to say. Last minute conversions are probably not going be recognized as those who believed and behaved properly all their lives. Those who believe they can jump aboard the heaven express at the last moment, are going to miss the train because of their blindness to the truth.

What is going to happen after the end time? Does everything just get destroyed? Lucky for man there is a rebirth of the Universe and earth. Science sums it up this way. When the Universe collapses in on itself, and condenses back into the super dense, super small particle, there will be another big bang, and the Universe will be born anew. Remarkably this agrees quite closely to what is written in Isaiah 66:22, "For as the new heavens and new earth, which I shall make, shall remain before me, saith the Lord, so shall your seed and your name remain.

The role of God as Alpha and Omega, the beginning and the end, has been explored in enough depth so that the average person can grasp the full impact of how true the Holy Bible speaks. It has been pointed out how everything came from God, and how everything has to return to God. There has been established that an end time is to come, and every person need prepare himself for that time.

There is a further question about God, and it has to do with the belief in multiple gods. To take a look at this question we need return to Isaiah 43: 10, "Ye are my witnesses, saith the Lord, and my servant whom I have chosen: that ye may know and believe me, and understand that I am he: before me there was no God formed, neither shall there be after me. God is declaring that he is the first and last God to be formed, and there has always been a wondering challenge to this.

In the first place, it has to be considered, What lies on the outside of the heaven Universe? God has established his domain with the boundaries of infinity and for ever, and as far as man knows, or can determine, or even conceive, there is nothing more. This means reality ends with infinity and forever. This also has to mean that God has used up all available space in existence. This means he is Master or Highest power of all space and time. Two considerations have to be looked at. There is nowhere for another god to exist without out God knowing about it. Our God is a jealous God, and he tells us in Exodus 20:3, Thou shalt have no other gods before me. It may seem this is an admission that other gods exist, but he is speaking of man created gods, idols, images, and the like. It extends to believing in gods controlling the waters, and the wind. The worship of stars, as in Greek mythology, the belief in reincarnation, and the power called upon by those practicing the Eastern religions, are also banned. Devil worship, voo doo, and mediums, and wizardry, are all a violation of God's commandment concerning other gods.

A logical question was asked of science, Could have more than one Universe have formed during the big bang? Scientists agree that if other universes formed during or after the big bang, that they were either too sparse with matter, and just drifted apart, or they were too dense, and collapsed in on itself. They go on further to say this about the physical Universe. For a Universe to have expanded for so long as this one has, without having its matter drift away, or becoming too dense so that it would collapse in on itself, required extra ordinary fine tuning. They do not admit that God had to do that fine tuning, but they rate the chance of this happening naturally as this. To achieve such a fine tuning would have the same odds as throwing a microscopic needle across the Universe, and scoring a bulls eye one centimeter in size.

It is thereby pretty certain that we are a one Universe system, and that brings up the question, if another god did happen to form? Any god that were to form would want his own kingdom, and since our God has used up everything in existence, where could the other god have his kingdom? If he were to exist in this Universe, he would either have to be subservient to our God, or he would have to be an adversary to our God. No god would want to be subservient to another god, and so that would just about make them adverse to one another. The role of adversary to our God is filled by the fallen arch angel, Lucifer, so there is no chance or place where another God could fit in. In Isaiah 45:5 and 6 is written, "I am the Lord, and there is none else there is no God beside me: I girded thee, though thou hast not known me: That they may know from the rising of the sun, and from the west, there is none beside me. I am the Lord, and there is none else. The concept that God is Alpha and Omega, the beginning and end, the first and last, has been explored, and in doing so, has advanced new thinking about how the Universe was created, and how everything in existence fits together. It has been established that there is to come an end time, and that we may be approaching that time, or are at least nearing the threshold of that time. It has also been revealed that we are a one Universe, one God system, and that means each individual has to re examine their philosophy and make the needed changes if they are to survive to the day of immortality. There is good advice in Isaiah 51:7, "Hearken unto me, ye that know righteousness, the people in whose heart is my law; fear ye not the reproach of men, neither be ye afraid of their reviling.

CHAPTER 3

Genesis of Earth

"This saith the Lord, The heaven is my throne, and the earth is my footstool: where is my house that ye build unto me? and where is the place of my rest? There has always been the wonder as to how many planets are in the Universe that could have life on them, and how many of these planets that do exist that might have intelligent life equal to man?

Science believes, and has discovered quite a few planets in orbit around different stars, and from this they conclude there are countless billions of planets in the Universe, and if only one out of every hundred developed the same as earth, there would be billions of planets with life on them, and of these if only one in a hundred had intelligent life they would still number in the millions. This is why science has set up a program to listen for radio signals over a million or more frequencies in hopes of picking up a single faint signal from an intelligent source. Another spearhead of investigation is aimed at establishing ancient life forms on planets such as Mars.

To most people this sounds like a reasonable theory, and a worthwhile venture, but the absolute truth is that earth alone is the only planet in existence with life upon it. That's a pretty bold statement to make against the endeavor of scientific exploration, but what is speculation in light of the truth?

God didn't just go into creating the Universe and the earth in a happenstance way, but with much more skill that will ever be found in an architect or engineer. When God measured out the heavens using his thumb and little finger, called spanning, he was at the same time setting up the dark nebula that would bring about earth, and the Milky Way galaxy. The setting at the beginning of the book of Genesis in the Holy Bible is this. The darkness in which God is going to create the physical Universe in is in place, and God is readying the objects in the Universe for firing up at one time. The temperature in this darkness has to be close to absolute zero, because during the assembling there is little to no molecular action. In the quadrant of the Universe where the Milky Way galaxy is to be formed is a cloud of dark dust. Now we go to the Scriptures. Genesis 1: 1, "In the beginning God created the heaven and the earth. This is a summary of what was covered under the Alpha and Omega chapter. Now God talks specifically about earth. Genesis 1:2, "And the earth was without form, and void.... This stage of earth means it was nothing but dust in the dark nebula, and the temperature within this nebula had to be just above the -400 degrees Fahrenheit, absolute zero, because the first thing to happen is that an electrostatic attraction comes into existence. This action is the same static that cling wrap works, and why a balloon can be made to stick on a wall. This requires some type of molecular and atom movement, so that temperature rise was critical for earth to begin forming. This rise in temperature had to come from God himself. The formation of the galaxy, by the law of descending order established that stars would have planets, and planets would have moons and so forth, so while earth was forming in its dark nebula, other planets had to be forming in other nebulas that would come to be galaxies. This removes the mystery of whether or not there are other planets in the Universe. The reason the earth is without form is because God is about to introduce the electrostatic attraction which will start its formation, but at the moment it is nothing. It is void or empty because there is only dust particles, and nothing has started forming. The next stage is that God raised the temperature enough for electrostatic attraction to take place, and this is where negative charged particles of dust moved to and joined to positive charged particles of dust. At first only two particles joined then each of those drew four more, and as it started to form the combined force became greater, drawing more and more dust particles. Science calls this the accretion stage of development. As the ball of dust grows the effect of gravity begins to work on the newly formed ball, starting to compress it into a tighter ball. In doing this a small amount of heat was generated, and this caused the gasses trapped in the dust to separate from the compressing dust. At last the ball of dust reached the second stage of development. A ball of dust layered with frozen gasses on its surface. This is what is indicated in Genesis 1:2, the next part of the verse, "...and darkness was on the face of the deep. The se layers of frozen gasses are very near the absolute zero temperature, and the gaseous planets of our own solar system testifies that this is a natural state. Some of our outer planets have frozen lakes and seas of methane, or other gasses. The reason they are layered is because of their different specific gravity's or weights, with the heavier gasses at the bottom, and the lighter gasses on top. This can be illustrated by the way carbon dioxide floats on water, but mercury sinks.

In the last part of the verse, "... and the Spirit of God moved upon the face of the waters. desc ribes an extremely important event. It is by God moving over the frozen gasses, and setting up the formula for liquid water. This formula, two volumes of hydrogen to one of oxygen, or by weight two parts hydrogen to sixteen of oxygen, and the union occur at a high temperature. This means that in the deep cold of space, nearly -400 degrees Fahrenheit, something had to raise the portions of hydrogen and oxygen enough to create water, and that is why God moved over the frozen gasses, and turned some into liquid water.

At the same time, earth has grown to be a sphere that is now completely covered with liquid water. Elsewhere in the Universe the formula has gone out for water, but it is debatable whether any formed of its own accord, or as science would have it evolved. In the Milky Way galaxy the formula and God's work probably did allow for water to come into existence on some of the planets, and possibly on earth's moon as well. This seems to be the thinking of science. They speculate the moon may have a little water inside it, and there is a possibility that Mars may have underground water. Only time will tell, but it can be stated with good cause that earth is the only water planet in existence in the whole Universe. There's a reason for it, and it is this. What good would it do to have planets with water on them, when the unique being man is to inhabit only the planet earth? God knows that man is bound to earth, because earth is the only planet set up by him to nurture and preserve man. God did not create multiple earth's and multiple populations of man. We are a one God, one Universe, one earth and one mankind system, and that's the truth whether or not we want to believe it.

At this stage, where earth is a sphere covered with water, two different scenes are about to unfold. Earth, because of gravity working on it is getting warmer, and has developed enough heat to keep the sub zero water from freezing. It may be also that because of the dissolving action of water, many of the frozen compounds were absorbed into the water, making the water an antifreeze solution, and keeping the water liquid. Given the properties of water as a dilution, and neutralizing agent, it is quite possible for this to occur. This is noted by how the sea is a highly concentration of saline minerals and metals. The sun, the moon, and the other planets are forming in the dark nebula, along with the other solar systems that is to make up the Milky Way galaxy. In the rest of the Universe the other galaxies are forming, nebulas are condensing into matter, probably the black holes are forming, and every object is beginning to feel the heavy effect of gravity. Remember, there is nothing present to offset gravity, so gravity is at its maximum strength throughout the Universe.

Now Genesis 1:3, comes into play. And God said, Let there be light: and there was light. The entire Universe burst into animation, and it started the Universe to begin to rotate around the center on its axis. This turning was slow at first, but as the speed built up, centrifugal force gradually lessened the effects of gravity throughout the whole Universe, and eventually they were equal, then afterward at the top of the speed, which must be at the present time, higher centrifugal force is causing the objects to move outward from the center, and is therefore stronger than gravity. This is the balance God has set throughout the whole creation, and it is a vital part of earth's creation.

Even though light is beginning to streak through the darkness of the Universe, creating Universal time, no light is as yet falling on earth from the sun or any other celestial source. The light shining down on earth is through a portal God has opened to heaven, and it is God's light shining down on earth. Consider that the nearest star is several light years away from earth, and the sun isn't yet ready to ignite so where else could light come from but God? Turn to Revelation 18: 1, and read, "And after these things I saw another angel come down from heaven, having great power, and the earth was lightened with his glory. In these formative years of earth God has things planned out the way he wants to get things on earth done, and he is personally involved with its formation. That is why his Spirit moved over the face of the waters to create them, because he had to set up the formula himself. Now he opens a portal to the heaven Universe so that his light shines down on earth, and the unequal heating causes the planet to rotate on its axis for the first time. This is explained in Genesis 1:4, "And God saw the light, that it was good: and God divided the light from the darkness. This is the first revolution of earth on its axis, and a comparison can be made to the automatic washer of today as it enters the spin cycle. When the washer enters the spin cycle it at first is very slow, but gathers speed until it reaches its highest revolutions per minute. Earth also, because of the uneven heating of the surface, began to rotate very slowly on its axis, and gathering speed as the heating and cooling took full effect.

Genesis 1:5, "And God called the light Day, and the darkness he called Night. And the evening and the morning were the first day. Time is based on a period of darkness followed by a period of light. God called the light day, and the darkness night, and in the first revolution the period of time we know as a day was created. How fast did the earth rotate that first time? How fast was it the second day? The earth like the automatic washer is in an acceleration phase, so there is no way to label it as twenty four hours or anything else. It is only a point of completion, and it runs from the time when earth was dust in a dark nebula to the time it first revolved on its axis to create the first day.

In Genesis 1:5 begins a new day, and with it a new development. The earth is accelerating in its rotation, and there comes a time when centrifugal force has become strong enough to hurl water from off the surface of the earth. God explains this, "And God said, Let there be a firmament in the midst of the waters, and let it divide the waters from the waters. This is easy enough to visualize. Like the water in an automatic washer in the spin cycle, the water is thrown outward, is collected and pumped into a drain. On earth the water is thrown off the planet but only goes as far as the centrifugal force can throw it, and we can come pretty close to estimating that distance.

We know that for all practical purposes that earth's atmosphere ends about 100,000 feet of altitude above the planet. We know also the highest clouds, the cirrus, meaning curly, and formed of ice crystals, are seldom higher than 40,000 feet. We also know that most clouds are at 20,000 feet and less with most of our weather occurring below 10,000 feet. It is then fair to say whatever went to 100,000 feet boiled off into space, and those at 40,000 feet are the upper reaches of the weather on the planet, so it is then pretty accurate to say the layer of water was somewhere between sea level and 20,000 feet. If a guess had to be made, the 10,000 foot level would seem reasonable. This gets us to Genesis 1:7, "And God made the firmament, and divided the waters which were under the firmament, from the waters which were above the firmament: and it was so.

The action of centrifugal force, from the planet's rotation, tried to throw all the water off the planet, but gravity opposed the centrifugal force, so only the excess water was thrown off the planet to form a layer of water about 10,000 feet off the planet's surface. The water in orbit around the earth cannot fall back to earth because of centrifugal force, and the water on earth is trapped on earth by the force of gravity. This point of equalization allowed for there to be the two layers of water, separated by the space in between. Now is Genesis 1:8, "And God called the firmament Heaven, and the evening and the morning were the second day.

In getting into the time element factors, and the way science figures earth's age, is to ask this. How long did it take for earth to make its first rotation? Surely it had to be more than twenty four hours. Now the planet's speed is high enough to throw water off the planet, so we have to believe it was much higher than today's speed or objects would still be flying off the face of the earth. So that would mean the planet's rotation was faster than the twenty four hours. What about the time element between these two events marking the end of the creation period or days. They had to be somewhere between the slowness of the first day, and the fastest of the day wherein the firmament was created. There is no way to say that it took so many years for earth to gather enough dust, have water come upon it, and make the first revolution. We have no idea of the time involved for the planet to gain enough speed to throw off the water to create the firmament, but what God is saying is the second day or period of creation is now completed. In comparison, looking at how much was included in the first day, as compared to the event in the second day, it would be logical to believe the first day was longer than the second day, but there is no proof of this being right.

God is now ready to begin the third day of creation, and this is where earth is going to separate from all other planets forming in the Universe. It's doubtful that any other water planets exist, and that makes earth distinctive, but on the third day a very major event is going to occur, and we read it in Genesis 1:9, 10 and 11, "And God said, Let the waters under the heaven be gathered together unto one place, and let the dry land appear, and it was so.

We need to go back to catch up what is happening as earth accelerates to its highest speed. The water is thrown off, but internally earth is being compressed so that the heat build up from gravity is starting to melt the interior of the planet. It is still gathering dust, and the dust it is gathering forms a good part of the silt in the oceans today, and the fact that stellar dust still falls on earth today, makes good sense that in the early days of earth, more dust came to earth from the still forming galaxy.

How did the dry land appear? The inner core of earth was just getting molten, and the next layer in was compressed dust, almost like shale. Enough pressure and heat hadn't yet built up to for igneous, or fire formed rock, so the outer layer of earth under the water was mud packed dust. In the centrifugal force, trying to throw things off the planet, this is the highest speed reached in earth's rotation, the top layers from what is the mantel today up surface was buckling because gravity was operating on the more dense shale like rock, and this made the land under material under the water break loose from where it was anchored to the denser rocklike formation beneath the earth. These great pieces of earth rose upward to float on the water, and are the continents of today. The geologic plates are ready to form, but aren't yet in action, because enough heat has not been generated internally in the planet.

Science would have you believe that earth was once all molten, gradually cooled, and then wind, rain, and volcanic action caused the rock to grind into powdery soil, and that isn't logical at all when it gets to figuring God in the picture. Why would God create stone, then have it ground back up into soil, when he had a rich soil to start with in the dust? Doesn't it make much more sense that he'd use the rich soil available at the time instead of going though all the antics of making rock, and then grinding it back into soil?

Science contends that all the continents were once joined together into a single land mass, and they eventually broke up and drifted apart, and according to the shapes they might have been together, but they broke apart and rose to the surface as continents, and not as a single land mass. Here's why. We read it in Genesis 1: 10, "And God called the dry land Earth; and the gathering together of the waters called he Seas: and God saw that it was good. Take note that he uses the plural seas, and not singular form sea. If one piece of land had risen to float on the water, you would have one island and one sea. It is only by having continents that the waters can be separated into seas, as they are today. The depressions from where these massive amounts of land broke loose from became the sea beds into which the waters flowed into to create the seas. Incidentally, when it says God saw that it was good, means that he was satisfied with the outcome.

Now we need go back and catch up with what is happening to earth in the intermediate time. The planet is heating up internally, and with that heating up, the frozen gasses in the material making up earth, is becoming liquid, and gasses, and these are escaping into the atmosphere, and it could be imagined that there were probably geysers of the gasses escaping from the earth. This could be compared to the natural gas wells, if they were not capped, and used, they would be geysers. What's happening is that with the escaping gasses from the earth, and the heat being generated from God's light, and from the internal heat of the planet, the water above the earth is changing into water vapor and mixing with the gasses escaping from the planet. This forms a dense foglike atmosphere which light can barely penetrate, but it creates a hot house atmosphere, hot and steamy.

This thick atmosphere cannot keep pace with earth's fast rotation, and being slower it begins to exert a dynamic braking action on the earth, trying to slow the earth. A wind is blowing because of the difference in speed between the two bodies. This braking action increases the heat on earth, and coupled with the heating by God's light shining down through the fog like atmosphere, it had to be similar to what we know the weather is like around the equator, only hotter, and denser. It is into this setting God is going to introduce the first life onto the planet. Here again is there stark disagreement between science and the Holy Bible.

Science claims all life, including plant life came from the sea, but by Scripture, the first life is going to be plant life, and he's going to create it on the land. Genesis 1: 11, 'And God said, Let the earth bring forth grass, and the herb yielding seed, and the fruit tree yielding fruit after his kind, whose seed is in itself, upon the earth: and it was so.

God said, "Let the earth bring forth... and that means the earth was endowed at that time with the ability to bring forth plant life. How did God accomplish this? It is estimated that in each cubic inch of soil, there are more than 5,000 different chemicals, bacteria, enzymes and other properties that allow plants to grow. This is what makes earth different from every other planet in the Universe, and the ability to bring forth vegetation is limited to earth as far as we know.

If evolution and the scientific model were used, then there would be no reason why every planet in our solar system and in the Universe to have life adapted to that particular planet, as life on earth is adapted to earth. That would mean that life should be abundant and teeming throughout the solar system and the Universe, but this isn't the case. Earth is the only planet known to have any life forms, and the answer is simple. God endowed and ordained earth to bring forth vegetation, and that endowment has limitations.

We know there is no plant life on the moon, and the soil of the moon is sterile. We know also that few plants live above the timberline on earth, and the timber line reaches about 20,000 feet.

The ultimate range of the life zone on earth then can only extend from about 30,000 below the surface of the sea to about 30,000 feet above the surface of the sea. That's a total of 60,000 feet or roughly 12 miles in depth. Most of the life is concentrated between sea level and 20,000 feet of elevation, and it is the same under the sea. This limitation keeps life from expanding to other planets.

When science paints the rosy picture of colonizing other planets, having outposts on planets like Mars under huge domed plastic domes, and growing food in a created atmosphere, it is just pure fantasy, and the reason is because God has not ordained other planets to produce and nurture life. Seeds taken from earth and planted in Martian soil probably wouldn't even sprout, but if they did, they would soon die thereafter, because the necessary enzymes, bacteria, and other wide variations of life needed for chemical breakdown and absorption, aren't present outside earth. This is also why man can never really expect to wander too distant from earth -- because they have to take their food along with them. Plants that were tried to be farmed in space also didn't pan out too well, and they keep hushed about that failure.

Again the question, Why would God create all these planets with vegetation when man is to be limited to two places, heaven and earth? It doesn't make good sense to believe he'd do it anyway. Now if Mars, Venus, and the moon were to have vegetation on them, then this would indicate that vegetation and the soil were part of the normal progression in the life and death of a planet or moon, but since the likeness ended with the descending order of things where stars would have planets, and planet moons, then we can be assured that the planets of other stars, are as barren as Mars, Venus, and Mercury, and that those having moons, despite the discovery of volcanic action on some, are only to be desolate landscapes without any life forms.

Might man someday plant the necessary ingredients into the soil of other planets to change the soil to life productive soil? The answer has to be no, and the reason is this. As each year goes by, earth's soil continues to lose its life producing and nurturing ability. That is why fewer and fewer new or unheard of species of plants are turning up. It goes right back to this time in Genesis when God said, Let the earth bring forth... , and the moment earth acted on that command, it began depleting itself of the ability to bring forth and nurture life. It could be compared to having a gigantic reservoir of gas, and as it is expended, there is no way to replace it. This is why destroying the forests, the grass, and other plant life further weakens and saps the planet's ability to bring forth and nurture plant life. The earth is getting well past its prime, and that means as time goes on, and man greedily destroys the vegetation of earth, the quicker the ability of earth to recover and nurture is depleted. This is something man knows about the oil deposits, the mineral deposits, and it's true about the earth's ability to nurture vegetation as well, but is there any slow down to the mad rush to gather more? In the case of forests, especially those around the equator, the land gives up too much of her ability to replace the vegetation life lost to such harvest. We witness this in the northern forests where forests now have to be fertilized to keep growing, and farm land is saturated with chemicals to make it produce crops. We constantly hear these are the renewable crops, the timber, and the grains, the vegetables, and the other crops harvested and quickly replanted. Look at the common sense approach the God gave us in Exodus 23: 10 and 11, "And six years thou shalt sow thy land, and shalt gather in the fruits thereof: But the seventh year thou shalt let it rest and lie still: that the poor of thy people may eat: and what they leave the beasts of the field shall eat. In a like manner thou shalt deal with thy vineyard, and with thy olive yard. If this advice were followed the earth would not be forced to deplete its life giving ability so quickly, and the land would remain fruitful for a longer period.

Look at the facts. The 5,000 or more bacteria and enzymes, and other things needed, like earthworms, are destroyed by the overuse of herbicides, and pesticides, and this creates sterility or unproductive soil. No one knows what destroys the necessary enzymes and bacteria, but by the things we use on the physical body to combat bacteria is usually of a chemical nature or a combination of chemicals. Isn't it reasonable to think that chemicals can also destroy the bacteria and enzymes in the soil?

The earth born to give life in the form of vegetation on this third day of creation was young and bursting fertility, so the grasses burst forth on the dry land, as God said. Take a look at the grass family. Grass for the most part lives fairly close to the ground, spreads through runners and seeds, and has a root system that prevents erosion of the soil by water. It is a tough plant, growing on any open patch of ground, and even in places such as cracks in the side walks of a city. In considering the wide varieties it ranges from the lowly cheat grasses to the cereal grains, wheat, rye, millet, corn, oats, barley, and a host of others. God knew well in advance that he was going to bring forth animal life on the planet, and also man, and for that reason he created grass as the fodder for the expected animal life. For this reason, there is no known poisonous grass in the world today.

The herbs grew bushy and higher than the grass, and their roots went deeper in the ground. They relied on their seeds riding on the wind to over spread the land of earth, and some of these today, such as the dandelion, and many of the flowering herbs still use the wind as the means to spread their seeds. They gave support and shelter to the grasses, and God put the herbs on earth as a supplemental diet for beasts and man. While no species eat one herb as a sole food source, there are a great many which after eating one type food, switches to nibble on an herb.

Herb sales in the world is growing by leaps and bounds, and it is slowly being found that many of man's maladies can be reduced or cured by natural herbs and medicine. There is this that has to be said about this. The act of selling herbs has become the same as selling the public a new car, so don't expect to save on doctor bills by going into herbal medicine treatments unless the person treating you is a proven expert with a proven track record.

While on the subject of cures of maladies, look at the causes of maladies. The medical profession is over taxed with cases to be healed, and the cause is relatively simple. Go back to eating food grown organically (without chemicals), stay away from packaged and canned foods in the supermarket, cook and bake everything from scratch so you know what you are eating, eat all you want of fresh vegetables and fruit, but avoid domestic meats of any kind, and of late, avoid eating fish, shell fish, and crustaceans because of the high metal contamination in these sources. If you do these things, you will be one of the few who will escape the ills of today, cancer, heart disease, tumors, and the rest.

God has given man the keys to successful living, and they are scattered throughout the Holy Bible, and if followed a good life can be had on earth yet, but it has to be done by separating from the worldly things that make you ill, and which contaminates your mind and good sense.

The fruit trees grew in groves, with their fruit falling to the ground, and new seedlings coming up from the pits in the fruit. Some of the trees, like the coconut palm, and the figs dropped some of their fruit, or pods into the waters, and the wind and waves carried them to distant lands to start a new population. It has to be remembered there are no insects, no birds, and no animals that can transport these seeds, so the water and wind were the only way they got transported. Fruit trees are in abundant variety, and outside a few, most are safe for man to eat. Many animals won't touch citrus fruits, and trees bearing nuts such as the horse chestnuts are better left alone by man, along with poison hemlock and other such plants. This is especially true with fungus or mushrooms.

The benefit of fruit in the daily diet has been lauded as the greatest food of all, supplying the natural fiber, sugars, and other nutrients. Fruit ranges from olives to bananas, and includes the nuts, anything that has its seed in its fruit.

It is hard to imagine why people have reverted to eating things chemically manufactured, genetically enhanced, or otherwise mutilated instead of fresh wholesome food grown on the individual garden plot. Commercially produced foods, are washed in solvents, treated chemically to retain freshness, and sprayed with chemicals to keep their appearance, but at what risk to the consumer? Just as the land is being poisoned by the over use of man made chemical compounds, so is man becoming afflicted through the over use of chemicals in the food chain.

The land which rose above the sea was lighter than the water, and therefore had to be the dust particles of the nebula, and not rock as dreamed by science. This rich soil is what makes up the river deltas, and the silt in the bottom of the sea, and it accounts for why there are some soil that is rich, and some soil that is poor for raising crops. The soil of eroded rock is not near so productive as is the soil from the rich dust of the dark nebula.

With the hot house temperatures, high humidity so that fog was ever present, and an atmosphere that was heavily concentrated with carbon dioxide, and nitrogen, the plant life flourished quickly into a jungle like setting in the rich earth. Plants grew rapidly and large, filling every space of ground available, and in profuse array of species. One trip to the tropical jungle belt of earth is enough to glimpse back to what the whole of earth was like at the end of the third creation day.

At the beginning of the fourth creation day Genesis 1: 14 is put into effect, "And God said, Let there be light in the firmament of heaven to divide the day from the night; and let them be for signs, and for seasons, and for days, and years.

This is the point in time in the creation sequence when earth is in orbit around the sun, but the sun has not yet ignited, and the moon is in orbit around the earth. Earth's orbit around the sun, like all the planets was nearly circular. What this did was allow earth the benefit of God's light on an even basis, and so there was only one season, and it had to be near what the conditions at the equator is today, about twelve hours of day, and twelve hours of dark, hot days and warm nights, and high humidity.

With the establishment of plants on the planet, earth's atmosphere is changing. The plants are busy converting the carbon dioxide over to oxygen, and many of the other lighter gasses are escaping into outer space, above the 100,000 foot level. As the plants converted the carbon dioxide to oxygen, the atmosphere began to clear, and the lighter atmosphere exerted less braking action on the planet because it was nearing the speed of the rotation of the planet. The atmosphere was being speeded up by the pull of the planet's rotation, and the planet was being slowed down by the drag of the atmosphere. The wind once raging over the planet's surface, began to subside, but at altitude they continued on. We experience these winds as the jet streams which generally flow from west to east, the same as weather patterns move from west to east. This due to the planet and the near atmosphere moving at nearly the same speed, but at altitude they are moving faster because the earth's rotation is still slowing, and because there is slippage, because of the fact the air is not a solid link. The upper air cannot respond to changes in speed as rapidly as the lower level of air.

This is viewed on the gaseous planets where winds at altitude around the equator of the planets can exceed 700 miles per hour, and the atmosphere is very turbulent and violent.

With the solar system ready, and the earth adorned with vegetation and an atmosphere, the sun is ignited. When the sun roared to life, there had to occur a flash over, and though this searing heat lasted only a short time, it was enough to scorch the surface of the inner planets, Mercury, Venus, and Mars, and earth's moon.

This flash over didn't affect earth heatwise because of the heavy blanket of atmosphere laden with water that covered earth. What did happen was that every planet was moved out of a circular orbit into an elliptical orbit, and this is seen today, by the inner planets having a more elliptical orbit than the outer planets. The orbit of Pluto, the farthest out planet, has nearly a circular orbit, but as the distance from the sun is decreased, the planets' orbits become more elliptical. This of course set up the seasons on the planet earth.

When God ignited the sun, he saw the sun was going to do everything he wanted it to do, so he closed the portal that he had opened to heaven, and this was like severing the umbilical cord, or the weaning away. From this moment on the planet earth was going to respond to the laws of physics, and not be subject only unto God's constant supervision.

There has to be a clarification of the firmament, and it is this. God uses the word heaven to describe, going out fom earth, the first space, between the surface of the earth, and about 20,000 feet altitude, heaven where the birds fly, then he uses heaven as outer space, and he uses heaven in reference to where he resides. Heaven on earth is always up, and that means our Universe is centered around God and centered in the Universe known as heaven. This is only possible by being the example of being a bubble within a bubble as explained in the previous chapter.

The day and night system was set up by the rotation of earth on its axis, and there is no way of telling how long a day this was, and the reason is this. A year or so back, all the clocks in the world was adjusted by one second to account for the slowing down of the planet's rotation, and science says this occurs about every ten thousand years. We are then pretty sure that the days of Adam and Eve were the same as the days we know, but accordingly the farther back in time we go, even at the rate of one second per ten thousand years, how fast was the earth spinning at the time the sun ignited? Its impossible to say, but it had to be a shorter time span than it is today. That is why saying earth is 4.6 billion years old is mostly a bunch of hooey, because there isn't any way to gage time under such varying conditions. Here is an illustration. When you bake a cake, you put the ingredients in a mixing bowl, add the liquid, and mix, then you bake it in the oven. Now, try to sort out each separate ingredient, and try to say it was this old when it got mixed, and this old when it got baked. There isn't any practical way to do this, and the carbon dating, and radiation dating used by science is just as much in error as most of their theoretical rhetoric.

Who has lived long enough to find the half life a compound rated at a million years? Or who was there to see the first carbon formed? The earth is as old as it is and the sun is as old as it is, and the Universe is as old as it is, and there is nothing more known for sure. No person outside of Christ was present at the birth of the Universe, earth, or man, so there is no real way for man to know these things. Did they take billions of years, or were they done like "poof"? What is known is that God does some things quickly, and other things are done slowly in man's view of them, but what about from God's view? Might not his view be much different from ours?

There is reason to believe, that some time was involved to get earth through the different stages, or creation periods or days, but since earth time wasn't created until the fourth day of creation, how can there be reference to it?

The time when the sun first shone down on earth, was the first earth day as we know it, because no one lived in the day when God's light from heaven shone down on earth from a portal between heaven and earth. Even then, there is no way we know for certain how long it took for the earth to make one revolution on its axis, but we can guess that its rotation was some faster than today.

We know the sun is for the day, and the moon for the night, along with the star light, but the phases of the moon creates the month, and our orbit around the sun sets the seasons and years. The signs that God said lights in the firmament were to be for us, is one we need pay attention to, because it is from what is happening in the Universe that predicts what is going to happen on earth. The star of Bethlehem announced Christ's birth, and the end time is going to be a time when stars or other heavenly bodies are going to play an important role.

We use the zodiac and other star groupings to depict the sky. In Greek mythology, and in other cultures, all have looked toward the stars as signs. As in most things, the use of stars and other celestial object by God to give us information has become perverted and misused to satisfy man's own egotism. God tells us in Isaiah 51:6, "Lift up your eyes to the heavens, and look upon the earth beneath: for the heavens shall pass away like smoke.

The return of Christ shall be from above, and we are reminded that we need to look upward to the heavens and God. It is doubtful there is a person alive who has eyesight, that has wandered out of doors into the night, that do not glance up to the sky. This seems to be a built-in reaction, and we do it as involuntarily as we breathe. Have you ever wondered why you look up?

The mystery of the Universe, and the mystery of God is ever present, and we look upward to see if we can figure it out. It must be we have an inner hope that in that one glance, or a long gaze, that understanding of the wonder of the Universe and God will be revealed to us. We associate with the fact that God is above us, somewhere in heaven, and that thought, even in the subconscious mind, causes us to lift our eyes toward God in silent awe and wonder. In the day, with only the sun, we lift our eyes to the sky to glimpse the weather, because our mind is usually too crowded with daily activities to take the time to view the blue paradise above, or the paradise we live on. When we lay on the beach, or on the grass and look up into the sky above, again our sight, mind, and attention focus on God, and the wonders he has created. No man can escape this relationship between man and the world he is born into.

With the establishment of the sun and moon in earth's sky, God called an end to the fourth day or period of creation. Science has come up with arbitrary periods of earth's formation, and they try to hold these to prove the theory of evolution, and the big bang, but of recent days, more and more scientists are becoming dissatisfied with the theory of evolution and the big bang theories, and have started searching for more satisfying theories. It is a strange calamity they will not start with the truth of the Holy Bible, God's word, and proceed from there. It has to be more than being stiff necked about the truth, and that means they must be under the influence and guidance of Satan, the father of all liars, and deceivers.

Science claims that life started on earth in the ocean, where the near constant lightning strokes caused some acids to string together, forming what science calls DNA. From this evolved all vegetable and animal life on the planet. It is science's contention because DNA is in essence the first building block to life, that they are right in this assumption, and have done laboratory experiments to prove that acids would string together in sea water with artificial lightning strikes taking place nearly constantly. Does this prove the scientific theory and model? The answer is no, and for this reason.

Consider that if God decided life would come onto the planet, and would be carbon based, and he knew the formula had to be general enough to produce life by the formation of acids linking together, the formula for DNA would be made earth wide. It doesn't seem reasonable he'd use DNA for animals, and another for plants. DNA is the formula for life, but is not life. Here's a practical application. Diamonds are carbon, but does that mean all carbon is a diamond? Carbon may have the potential to become a diamond, but only under specific temperatures and pressures. DNA has the potential of life, but without God acting on the DNA, it is like the carbon, not to be a diamond unless other things occur. This is why everything on earth is DNA oriented and based.

The reason life on earth is carbon based is because it is abundant, and God used that base and DNA to create life on earth, and he did it by what is written in Genesis 1:20, "And God said, Let the waters bring forth abundantly the moving creature that hath life, and fowl that may fly in the open firmament of heaven. With these words God en dowed the waters of earth, the seas, to bring forth life using carbon as a base, and DNA as the formula, but it is in his blessing that the sea itself is given the ability to provide the spark of life. At the onset, life in the warm seas flourished in a spectacular array and splendor. Life burst forth in unchecked abundance, and many of those creatures are still living today, although they are no longer of gigantic size. The sea was a natural nursery, full of the needed minerals and acids needed for rapid growth. By this time the plants of earth had also began to flourish in the water, and this can be considered the time when evolution came into play. Some of the plants living near the shore, such as the marsh grasses, probably started changing due to the mineral and acid change taking place in the sea, and this caused a change in the plants. There is no definitive way to say the first plants were slime in the sea, nor can it be said the plants on earth somehow moved to the sea. It is more likely that plankton, the amoebae, and other cross strains between plant and animal were created in the sea under God's blessing that the sea could bring forth life. Most of these cross species between animal and plant are gone, from earth, but some might yet remain hidden in the depths of the oceans.

The point is, God blessed and endowed the seas with the ability to produce life, and it did so in abundance, but like everything, that power is becoming spent as the planet ages, and the sea is no longer as productive as it once was. Fewer and fewer new species are emerging, and more and more species are becoming extinct. If this trend were to continue, eventually the seas would again be barren and sterile. The same can be said for earth. Plant species go extinct, while few new species come onto earth, and over time, the earth like the sea would become barren and unproductive, as the planet approaches its life span end.

The theory of evolution is based upon the DNA theory of life on earth, and science tries to apply this to the other planets in the Universe, and that's like trying to put a fender off one make car onto another make car. It just doesn't fit. The carbon and water based life here with the formula of DNA is applicable to earth alone. If evolution were the cause of life, then Mars, and the other planets and moons in our solar system, and the countless planets and moons in other systems would flourish with life adapted to their environment, the same as earth is adapted to earth's environment. If DNA is the formula here on earth to work in conjunction with water and carbon, why not on a planet with high silicon and an acid availability, and use of a different formula to produce life, say in a sea of methane? That also should produce a life form if evolution is a fact. If evolution were the cause of life on earth, then it would be likely it worked throughout the whole Universe, and the resulting life would be from the more common elements of every different body of land and sea, regardless of the compounds involved. Since this isn't the case, evolution can be discounted as the cause of life, and the ability of giving life has to revert to God as being the source.

These creatures of the seas, the fish, and shell fish, the crustaceans and all other species were cold blooded, with the exception of the whales. This time in earth's history is the age of the dinosaur, and like so much else of science's determination, they have missed the boat on the dinosaur as well. In their dissertation of evolution, they have theorized that birds came ftom the reptiles, and this isn't true at all. The birds of those days are the birds of today, the shore birds such as the gulls, terns, albatross, the geese, ducks, pelicans, storks, ibis, and the whole host that we know as water fowl today. These creatures were to inhabit a specific niche in nature, as were the other creatures in the sea, and even today these birds stay near water.

This isn't to say there were not flying reptiles, but the feathered birds, with the webbed feet, have changed little from the early days of earth. The whales also have remained aloof to change, and still haunt the seas as they did in the early seas.

The most remarkable animal was the dinosaur of this time, and he was a water animal, huge in size, and needed the water for buoyancy in the same way the hippo of today uses the water as a buoyancy for his body. These beasts were cold blooded and roamed the warm waters of earth, maybe nesting on land even as the alligators, and sea turtles nest on shore, but spend a good portion of their lives in the water.

The dinosaurs required huge amounts of vegetation to support their body, and they spent their time browsing on the grasses, herbs, and fruit trees bordering the shores. They didn't need much for brains, because food was abundant, and there were no predators. The old bunk about the T Rex being a flesh eater is strictly speculation on science's part. They use the formation of the teeth as evidence they were designed for ripping meat, but it is more likely they were used to strip the husks off nuts like the coconut, and to crack open the hard encasement of the nut to get at the meat.

In animals that are vegetation eaters, the molar is important, but in the age of the dinosaur the plants were huge, and required a lot of strength and ripping power to shred the vegetation into something to ingest. We see this in the elephant, where they tear down acacia trees with their trunks to get to the foliage. But couldn't we misconstrue this long nose as a method to crush animals for food like the boa constrictor?

It doesn't seem reasonable that God is going to create predators to feed on prey animals when he's trying to get life established on the planet. It doesn't add up as being sensible or logical.

Therefore the first animals had to be vegetarian, and they fed on the lush vegetation of earth, and it need be remembered that all earth at this time is a jungle like setting, warm, humid, and lush.

The earth is now well established in its elliptical orbit around the sun, and is on an elevated plane rather than a flat plane, and earth is settling into a system of seasons. The two poles begin seeing the changes first, growing colder, and ice begins forming. The climate of earth is just starting to change, and the change is very significant. Up until this time, earth has been like a hot house, but now the atmosphere is experiencing a change in temperature, and there is the slightest wisps of clouds high up, where the cirrus clouds are formed of ice crystals. Until this time, there was enough heat in the air to prevent clouds, but with this change, earth is moving toward a cooler climate, with seasonal changes. The practical thing of this is that the swing from being tropical is going to be radical, and earth is going to go right into an ice age because the change occurs too fast to be moderate.

The dinosaurs that were ranging far north and south of the equator were the first to experience the change, and the change was rapid. Everyone is aware that any reptile needs to warm up in the sun before they can become very active, and the dinosaurs weren't any different. With the change of temperatures, those of the north probably tried to move south to warmer climes, following their food source as the vegetation withered and died in the colder temperatures. Then as the cold swept southward, more and more animals died, and with the waters becoming colder in the northern latitudes, the animals became more sluggish, and were unable to feed for as many hours as they needed.

The earth itself, now molten in the center and with volcanoes erupting to relieve the inner pressures, began changing the land masses. Meanwhile, the tectonic plates began movement. New lands thrust up as mountains, and old lands sank into deep valleys and depressions. The volcanic ash spewed into the atmosphere darkened the sun for days and weeks, causing a further cooling to the earth's atmosphere.

As the earth's climate changed the dinosaurs lost interest in mating, and spent the majority of their time trying to wrest enough food from the land for survival. The dinosaurs' main purpose in life was to eat the lush vegetation and groom the earth, and they did it well. With the seasons established on earth, the weather is now ready to plunge from tropical to an ice age, and the poor dinosaur couldn't keep pace, not could it adapt. It therefore starved and perished by not being able to react to the changing environment.

The birds of feather were well equipped for the climate change, but it must be remembered that there is not yet a system established for condensing the moisture in the atmosphere into rain or snow, so freezing fog and heavy dew were what watered the land areas of earth during this time. This is explained in Genesis 2:6, "But there went up a mist from the earth, and watered the whole face of the ground.

With the fourth day of creation drawing to a close, God has the planet ready for his next step in bringing man to the planet, and that is to establish the minimal form of life. The dinosaurs couldn't make the rapid changes needed to survive earth's rapidly changing climate, so on the fifth day Genesis 1:25 becomes the word. "And God said, Let the earth bring forth the living creature after his kind, cattle and creeping thing, and beast of the earth after his kind: and it was so.

God didn't change from the formula of DNA, water, and carbon to produce life, but what he did is give earth itself the ability to bring forth new life onto the planet. Thus the soil of earth can bring forth plants and animals, and the seas can bring forth the cold blooded creatures.

These first mammals, included such animals as the cave bear, and the saber toothed tiger, but again they are said to be carnivores by science, and this isn't true. Here is what is said about all animals produced on earth so far, up to this time of creation. It is contained in Genesis 1:30 "And to every beast of the earth, and to every fowl of the air, and to everything that creepeth upon the earth, wherein there is life, I have given every green herb for meat: and it was so.

The greatest beasts on earth have always been vegetarians, and even the greatest whales in the ocean are plankton eaters. This is why it is more logical for the dinosaurs to have been herbivores rather than carnivores.

The vegetation on earth changed as the climatic conditions changed, but this wasn't do to evolution as science imagines, but came from the ability of the earth to fill the vacant niches in the vegetation. Cactus and other desert plants began to dot the barren and poor soil of the more arid lands, grasses, flowers and herbs thrived in the meadow lands, and the conifers began inhabiting the colder reaches of the planet. It doesn't take much speculation to disbelieve that trees came from moss, or algae. It does seem logical to believe that the earth brought forth the vegetation and the animals adapted to the different climate conditions of the planet as the niches appeared. This is a much more sensible approach than believing that something like a frog came up out of the ocean and evolved into a land animal.

The fact that few new animal species are being found on earth is not because they have all been discovered, but rather that earth has run its course in the ability to produce animals to fill the niches as they occur. The productivity of the earth to produce animals and new species of plants is waning to where few if any more will ever be produced by the earth, and when an animal occupies a specific niche on earth goes extinct, it is not being replaced, and the space becomes either a void, or other animals adapt to cover the spot. Suppose for a moment that all herbivores on the planet went extinct. When the dinosaurs faded out they were replaced by the mammals, but now the earth is unable to fill the vacancies left by the extinction of all herbivores, and the whole ecology of earth is changed and man himself is threatened. The act of bringing carnivores or predators was in response to overpopulation in some species. Insects began to flourish more than the other animals, and this is known today, that insects occupy the largest part of the world's environment. While the early fowl of the air depended on fruit and nuts, thought has to be given to those like the parrot, and macaws with the curved beaks which had to be among the earliest birds, and which still eat fruit and nuts. Then there are the geese which eat grass, and this goes a long way to substantiate quite well that the early animals and birds did subsist on fruits and vegetation.

There's a added note to how the earth and the sea could spawn life using the formula and base God laid out to them, and it is in the possibility of the Loch Ness monster. This serpentine, or dinosaur looking beast, if proven true, could be the relic of the dinosaur era, like the alligators, snakes, frogs and other cold blooded animals on earth today, or it could be the last of a new species of animal spawned by the sea. The same might be said of the land animals called the Sasquatch or the Yeti. These animals may be the last species to ever be produced by the earth to fill the niche left by the great flood of Noah's time. It's just something to think about.

With the mammals established on earth, God is about mid way the sixth day or creation period, and the planet is ready for his highest and best achievement, the introduction of man onto the earth. God is now ready to enact what is written in Isaiah 43:20, "The beasts of the field shall honor me, the dragons and the owls: because I give waters in the wilderness, and rivers in the desert, to give drink to my people, my chosen.

With that thought in mind, we turn to a new chapter in the history of earth, the populating of earth with man. God's highest achievement.

CHAPTER 4

Genesis of Man

The genesis of man begins in the afternoon of the sixth day or period of the creation, and this event has caused more calamity and misunderstanding than any preceding event in the history of earth. Some of the mystery can be wiped away by asking: If man is nothing more than an animal, then why was he afforded a different status on earth than any other animal? Then too is the question: If man isn't more than an animal, why go through all the work of creating the Universe, and earth? Why didn't God just stop after he created the heaven Universe with all the angels and beasts he has there?

Obviously, there has to be more to man than just being an animal, and it goes back to when God formed himself In him was the first life, and what greater thing could God do but the share that life with other beings? The spiritual beings in heaven were created, and the greater majority of these are the angels, or messengers of God. We don't know how many angels there are in existence, but we do know there are seven arch angels, or boss angels that look over the regular angels. Among the arch angels was Lucifer, and Lucifer was not only the most powerful angel, he was also the most beautiful, and he plays an important part in the overall plans of God.

In attendance around God, are his close in associates, there are the twenty-four elders, and the beasts that fly about the throne of God. These are the incorruptible and the reason they are incorruptible is because evil cannot exist in the close proximity to God, and these associates are under the protection of God, making them immune to sin, or entirely holy, unable to sin against God.

The next level of government are the seven arch angels, and they are known as the sons of God, but not to be confused with the Son of God, one of the entities making up God himself We know the names of some of these arch angels. There is Lucifer, Gabriel, and Michael. These arch angels have the power to supervise the ordinary angels, and though we have no idea how many angels serve God, they must be fairly numerous to have seven arch angels over them.

Lucifer was created as the most beautiful arch angel, and he had the power to act in God's name, and accomplish things, more or less they way a superintendent or CEO of a corporation can operate within certain boundaries on his own without having to consult with the owners of the corporation. Because of his high position in the realm, Lucifer was allowed access to places that were off limits to the other angels, places where normally only God went. We read about Lucifer in Ezekiel 28:13 through 17. "Thou has been in Eden the garden of God. It's important to remember this verse, because it has a great bearing in the creation of man. "Every precious stone was thy covering, the sardius, topaz, and the diamond, the beryl, the onyx, and the jasper, the sapphire, the emerald, and the carbuncle, and gold: the workmanship of thy tabrets, and of thy pipes was prepared in thee in the day that thou wast created. It is uncovered here that God evidently likes music, because here is an angel with ability to make music using pipes, quite probably a flute like instrument, and tabrets, which are small cymbals.

In verse 14 is his appointment to office, "Thou art the anointed cherub that covereth: and I have set thee so: In this God is saying that Lucifer is appointed as his superintendent, and he is the most powerful being in existence in heaven outside God himself, and the three entities that make up God. "Thou wast upon the holy mountain of God; thou hast walked up and down in the midst of the stones of fire. It's pretty obvious that Lucifer had full run of heaven, from the holy mountain of God, to hell and the stones of fire. Remember, Hell as a place of torture isn't established yet, because there isn't any reason for it. Evil hasn't yet come into existence.

Throughout the creation of the physical Universe, Lucifer went about instructing the other arch angels what needed to be done. The things the arch angels couldn't do, Lucifer did, using the authority granted him by God to do things in his name.

In this way, when God measured out the Universe, instructed Lucifer as to how the heavens were to be laid out, and they were the general commands, "Let there be... and Lucifer knowing what God had in mind, saw to it that the project was completed.

There came a time however, when Lucifer, looking over the creation, and seeing what he had accomplished under God's authority, began to think that God was just a figure head, and he was really the mastermind, because he made everything mesh together and work. This is what is expressed in verse 15, "Thou was perfect in thy ways from the day that thou wast created, till iniquity was found in thee. Iniquity is wickedness or violence, an act against God. What was the wickedness? We read about it in Verse 16, "By the multitude of thy merchandise they have filled thee with violence, and thou hast sinned: therefore I will cast thee as profane out of the mountain of God: and I will destroy thee, 0 covering cherub from the midst of the stones of fire. Lucife r, meaning light bearer, must have been an awesome sight to behold in his position of the highest arch angel. There has to be a return to Isaiah 45:7, and read, "I form the light, and create evil From this it has to be construed that at some point in time, God decided he would have to somehow measure the devotion of the life he created, and to do this, he created evil. This was to weigh out and judge all things he created, giving each individual angel the right to choose between good and evil. God's plan is this. If everything was to stay within his near vicinity, they could not come under the influence of anything evil, because they were shielded by God's power that wouldn't allow evil to exist in his local presence. But then, if everything was created where there was no choice, everything would be an enslaved creation, and not with liberty or freedom. God therefore created the arch angels and angels with the ability to choose between good and evil, as a means of judging their true love, adoration, and loyalty.

Then in Ezekiel 28:17 is written, "Thine heart was lifted up because of thy beauty, thou hast corrupted thy beauty by reason of thy brightness: I will cast thee to the ground, I will lay thee before kings, that they may behold thee. This simply states Lucifer became vain, believing he could unseat God and become like God, the Highest power in existence. This is recorded in Isaiah 14: 12, 13, and 14. "How art thou fallen from heaven, 0 Lucifer, son of the morning! how art thou cut down to the ground, which didst weaken the nations! For thou hast said in thine heart, I will ascend into heaven, I will exalt my throne over the stars of God: I will sit also upon the mount of the congregation, in the sides of the north: I will ascend above the heights of the clouds: I will be like the most High.

Earlier it was said that if another god had been formed he would either have to be subservient to our God, or be an adversary to our God. Here is Lucifer deciding he is another god, and is going to try and oust our God, and take over heaven, and all that is in it. This is to have a remarkable effect on earth during the period of man's creation. It starts in Genesis 1:26, "And God said, Let us create man in our image and likeness. What precipitated God to say those words, when he could have just made man without comment? He didn't say, let us make a cow like this, or a horse like that, so why did he say that man was to be in his image and likeness?

There are two very basic reasons, and they both have to be explored to the fullest extent. The first is that at the very beginning, God wanted to replicate himself, and while he could do this in heaven, he evidently wanted to express himself in more than just the one medium of heaven. That's why he laid out the Universe, the earth, and man. By creating man in a physical form, in his own image, on earth, and by giving man also a spiritual body, he was fulfilling his highest expectation, a replica of himself in more than one medium or form.

The second reason God might have said, Let us make man in our image and likeness... is because he has seen man on earth, and was displeased with what he saw, and therefore made the statement. This by Scripture becomes quite clear as the evidence unfolds, but the question is, Where did the men already on earth come from?

It has to be that Lucifer in his quest to rival God decided that the way to do this was to beat God to the punch in bringing man onto the planet earth. It has to be remembered that Lucifer was second in command under God, and he knew God's plan down to the tiniest details, but even in knowing those plans in detail didn't give him the benefit of knowing God's mind in the creation mode. It worked like this. Suppose you are told to draw a picture of a circle by using a continuous line going from a single point and returning to the same exact point. What would your circle look like? Surely not exactly like the one pictured by the person asking you to draw the circle, because you can't read that person's mind, nor conceive what he ideates.

Lucifer knew God was going to create man, and he had a rough idea of what man was supposed to look like, but he couldn't imagine what God was thinking man should be, and since Lucifer only had power to create the beasts of the land, by using God's word, he usurped that power and brought forth man which we call primitive man.

Primitive man was man like, but did not have the Spirit of God within him, so he was for all practical purposes an animal or beast. Here's what happened. Lucifer decided he would rival

God, and he was urged on by some of the ordinary angels under him. A full one third of the ordinary angels in the realm joined Lucifer in his rebellion against God. Lucifer then decided that he needed to have his own realm, and what better way to achieve that than bring forth man who would worship him as a God.

Lucifer then brought primitive man onto the planet, and when he walked and talked with the people he brought to earth, and taught them how to use fire, make tools, he did so as the shining angel that his name is given to him, Lucifer, the light bearer. Consider for a minute if you today met with a shining angel who could perform miracles before your eyes, and do great wonders in front of you, wouldn't you believe he might be a god? How can we imagine this to be true? The best evidence is in the discoveries made in South America, where pictographs show men with something that looks like space helmets, and acting as a god. Science speculates the natives were trying to depict the coming and going of alien astronauts, and that the massive drawings on top of plateaus were landing fields of these astronauts. It is more likely, since life is limited only to earth, that the helmet looking affair is to depict the light being emitted by Lucifer, and since he could go to and from heaven, the fields were laid out as a sign of worship to him.

The secret of building perfect monuments like the pyramids throughout the world, the statues of stone found on some islands, and the ability of these early people to engage in looking at stars, all are based upon their believing that the god which brought them on to earth, and who sometimes left, would again return, and these monuments were used to track the direction he left, and from where he might return.

When God arrived on earth, and found what Lucifer had done, and how he had usurped his power, God was angry with Lucifer and stripped him of his job as superintendent, and declared that he would be the symbol of all that is wicked and evil. There's this to think about. God would not condemn Lucifer for merely thinking he was as good as God, but he condemned him when Lucifer made the bold move to establish his own realm with the idea of ousting God from his own throne. Lucifer had to put his plan into action before God would condemn him, and that action was bringing the primitives onto earth to rival God's plans for man.

It is known there are three major races in the world today, and many sub races, and from what is known by science, the Black race, or Negroid race is the oldest known race in the world, and they originated in Ethiopia. What science offers as proof is the fossilized remains of a woman called Lucy, and she is the oldest fossil of man in existence. It is then pretty apparent that life started first in Ethiopia, and that the Black or Negroid race is the oldest race on earth. This means also that they must be some of the people Lucifer brought to earth by usurping God's power.

The Mongoloid race, or Asian people were the second group of people brought to earth by Lucifer, and the evidence is in the fact that China boasts a history of 10,000 years, whereas Adam and Eve were created 7,000 years ago. The accuracy of the Chinese history is born out in the fossil of the Java man, and since that discovery, more discoveries have come that collaborates Chinese history.

At the mid point on the sixth day of creation, God saw these people and declared, Let us make man in our image and likeness, and he took away Lucifer's authority to act in his name. Lucifer was then stripped to be only another arch angel.

We now look at Genesis 2:7, "And the Lord God formed man of the dust of the ground, and breathed into his nostrils the breath of life; and man became a living soul. In this scenario, man was created in God's image physically, and then given the Spirit of God, by God breathing the spirit into Adam's nostrils. This made Adam a physical and spiritual animated copy of God himself. After God had created Adam he looked around for a place to isolate him from the primitives that lived in the area. Now Genesis 2:8 comes into play. "And the Lord God planted a garden eastward in Eden: and there he put the man he had formed. The whole earth was still a garden, and there were no carnivores which would endanger Adam, so why did God hide him away in the garden?

We get an inkling of it in Genesis 2: 11. Out of Eden ran a river which watered the garden, and from there it was parted into four rivers, and while it is uncertain, the garden of Eden must have been near Mount Ararat where the Halys river, the Araxes, the Eurphrates, and the Tigris parted into four heads. Undoubtedly, the river beds have changed from that time, and the names of the rivers have changed, but there's enough description in the Holy Bible to give us some clues about it. Genesis 2: 11, "The name of the first river is Pison: that is it which compasseth the whole land of Havilah, where there is gold. This has to be Halys river running northwest toward Troy. Genesis 2:12, "And the gold of that land is good: there is bdellium and the onyx stone. There would be little use in mentioning this if there weren't people there to inhabit the land and use the materials mentioned. So this area had to be populated and the people had the ability to work metals like gold and bdellium, and could cut stone like the onyx.

Genesis 2:13, "And the second river is Gihon: the same is it compasseth the whole land of Ethiopia. This river has to be the mighty Nile river because it is the major river running south to water Ethiopia. There must have been some connection between a branch of the Euphrates river and the Nile at one time so Ethiopia would be part of the garden scene.

Genesis 2:14, "And the name of the third river is the Hiddekel: that is it which goeth toward the east of Assyria. And the fourth river is the Euphrates. The Araxes rivers flows east toward where Assyria must have been at the time, and the

Eurphrates is still known today. At best this is only an educated guess at the spot of the Garden of Eden, and though science has tracked ancient river beds through a good portion of the lands in the middle east, none have proved to be worthy of being the place where the garden of Eden was located.

It should be noticed more explanation is given the rivers of Havilah and Ethiopia than the remaining two because these two lands were populated, the Negroid in Ethiopia and the Mongoloids in Havilah. Adam, being the new Caucasian race, was then isolated from the other two races because God wanted to instruct and teach him to be a form of God.

To stay in continuity, we go now to Genesis 1:28, "And God blessed them, and God said unto them, Be fruitful and multiply and replenish the earth, and subdue it This is God speaking to Adam and Eve, and it has to be put in comparison of what God tells the animals in 1:22, "And God blessed them and said, Be fruitful, and multiply, and fill the waters in the seas, and let fowl multiply in the earth. To the animals he uses the word fill, and this indicates it is a first time population. But to Adam and Eve he says, replenish, which means refill, and not fill, as a original time. This means Adam and Eve are to replenish the earth with their species, and this means doing away with the primitives brought to earth by Lucifer.

While this may seem racist and cruel, it is only an attempt to straighten out the mess science and society has heaped upon itself without adequate knowledge of what God has told us. It could be supposed that Adam and Eve were to multiply, but at this stage, it has not been decided how this reproduction was to be accomplished. Eve was taken out of Adam, and this proves there are more ways to reproduce that by having sexual relations, even though it ended up that way.

The reproduction God might have had in mind could have been something like the way a cell divides, or by natural cloning, or any other way he deemed he wanted it done.

Reproduction of the beasts, and of primitive man was already set in the way reproduction takes place and is as it is in animals today. Even given the fact of how reproduction takes place in man today, there is still the ethic that the physical body of man is the temple of God, and that man is to confine himself to one mate, in marriage, with the blessing of God, and that makes the sexual act holy in marriage, and a sin outside of marriage.

Adam and Eve were supposed to replenish the earth, and it probably meant that Adam and Eve's line, the Caucasian, was going to continue on, and God was going to let the primitives die out, even as animals die out to extinction. What happened changed the whole chain of events, and there is this to say about things. It has to be understood that God, who was newly formed, knew a lot, but there were things he had to try with in experimentation, and when he came to life forms he did this in a startling array. God first used cold-blooded animals to populate the earth because the furred mammals would have suffered tremendously in the heavy heat and humidity, but this was perfect for the cold-blooded beasts. At the same time, God put whales, warm-blooded animals, in the seas because he knew eventually earth would cool, and the cold-blooded animals couldn't continue on, so he was proving out the warm-blooded mammal plan at the same time he was creating the cold-blooded animals that would first populate the earth.

It could be said that things like the mosquito, flies, gnats, and other pests of animals and man were at first not given to being pests, but provided some beneficial service to the environment, perhaps like the flies who pollinate plants in cold places where bees cannot operate. They later were used by God to pester man into regretting his sinful ways, and this is evident by the hordes of locusts that destroyed grain crops, mosquitoes that brought pestilence and diseases, and insects like mites, ticks, and lice to harass man. But it can also be said, that man will not turn away from wickedness and evil.

What happened next in the history of man concerns God stripping away of Lucifer's power, and made him the symbol of all that is wicked and evil. Lucifer then began to undergo a change in looks and temperament, and we see what happens when this occurs to man in Psalm 39:11, "When thou with rebukes dost correct a man for iniquity, thou makest his beauty to consume away like a moth: surely every man is vanity. Selah. When a person is rebuked for his sins, his countenance falls away, and his demeanor and looks change toward the ugly, because of the vanity within mankind. The word Selah means so be it, and the verse strikes home that man surely is almost incapable of accepting punishment, even if he is wrong!

In Satan the vanity stripped away some of his beauty, and he began changing from an arch angel toward a red dragon. This was a gradual change, and although the snake gets a bum rap from what is interpreted in Genesis 3:1, it has to be remembered a serpent isn't only a snake, but applies to the lizard family as well.

Most misinterpretation starts from Genesis 3:1, and goes on in 3:14, "And the Lord God said to the serpent, Because thou hast done this, thou art cursed above all cattle, and above every beast of the field; upon thy belly thou shalt go, and dust thou shalt eat all the days of thy life. The lizard is both a serpent and it goes with its belly also upon the ground, and then the description continues in verse 15, "And I will put enmity between thee and woman, and between thy seed and her seed; it shall bruise thy head, and thou shalt bruise his heel. It is a known fact that the saliva in a lizard is just as fatal as a strike from a snake, and the giant monitor lizard, known as a dragon, actually stalks and eat humans. The women and children of that land are not only deathly afraid of these lizards, but often fall prey to them.

In Revelation 12:3 is recorded, "And there appeared another wonder in heaven; and behold a great red dragon having seven heads and ten horns, and seven crowns upon his heads. This depiction serves in two ways. It shows Satan as a dragon at the head of nations on earth, and the Chinese dragon may be patterned after they viewed Satan after his change, and shortly after he was in the garden of Eden. The Mongoloids were his people, and it's only fair to say that he continued to walk among them after being stripped of his position and power by God. He was still a very powerful angel, and that has continued right on down through history until the present time.

When he was in the garden of Eden Lucifer still stood upright, and Eve saw him spiritually as an angel of light. We read how Lucifer can do this in II Corinthians 11: 14, "And no marvel; for Satan himself is transformed into an angel of light. This was part of the changeover from being an angel of light to the great red dragon to symbolize everything wicked and evil. God then changed Lucifer's name from Lucifer to Satan, which means adversary, and God more or less nicknamed him the Devil. If you remove the dee from devil you have evil, which is what Satan the Devil symbolizes.

There is another point that has to be made here and it is that the arch angel Lucifer after his full transition to Satan should be referred to as Satan and the Devil, and not Lucifer, because Lucifer, the light bearer was an angel, and not a red dragon and serpent. When he brought the primitives to earth in opposition to God, he was still an angel of the Lord, and he did it using God's word, so it is incorrect to say or believe these primitives were of Satan or the Devil. They were in fact formed out of the authority God had granted Lucifer for bringing animal life to the planet, and because of this, God decided to accept them into the family of man, as will be shown.

Satan appears to Eve in the garden, and taunts Eve by asking, "Didn't God say you could eat of every tree of the garden? Eve replies in Genesis 3:2, "And the woman said unto the serpent, We may eat of the fruit of the trees of the garden:

But of the fruit of the tree which is in the midst of the garden, God hath said, Ye shall not eat of it, neither shall ye touch it lest ye die.

Consider what is said. God has two trees in the garden that would directly affect Adam and Eve. The first is the tree of knowledge, and the second is the tree of life. Why would God put those trees in the garden if he wasn't going to let them eat of them? The clue is that up to this time, Adam and Eve saw God spiritually, and this can be likened to how you dream. You see, even though your eyes are closed. Adam and Eve could do everything they wished by spiritually seeing everything in the garden, and this is emphasized in Genesis 2:25, "And they were both naked, and were not ashamed. Think about this. When a newborn baby comes along, there isn't any shame in them for a couple of years, because they are not aware of their sexuality, and they could care less whether they are dressed or not. Their innocence is exactly the same innocence that Adam and Eve had before they ate the forbidden fruit.

In Eve, Satan sees a weakness, that of being gullible, and according to how many people are deceived on earth today, he's still at it in good form. In Genesis 3:4, "Ye shall surely not die. Now this to Eve was something, because God told her she shouldn't even touch it lest she die; now Satan is telling her she won't die.

Eve in weighing this out was gullible, not realizing for a minute that God wasn't speaking of the moment of eating that she would die, but that in eating of the fruit of the tree of knowledge, she would be denied the fruit of the tree of life which would give her immortality, and she would then be tied to a life span, as everything in creation is tied to a life span.

Satan then butters her up some more in Genesis 3:5, "For God doth know that in the day ye eat thereof, then your eyes will be opened, and ye shall be as gods, knowing good and evil. Satan knew full well that God was going to teach Adam and Eve how to be little Gods, the children of God. First though, they had to be educated how to live a holy life, doing only good, and the best way to learn this was in the absence of evil. This time for getting educated has been postponed until Christ returns and sets up a 1000 year government, where there will be no evil on the planet, and men will learn only goodness. After that time has passed, when men have had enough schooling in being holy, Satan will be loosed, and allowed to come and tempt man again. Think of how much easier it would have been for man to have learned what God wanted Adam and Eve to learn in the first place, learning to be holy and righteous as he himself is.

We continue with Genesis 3:6, "And when the woman saw that the tree was good for food, and was pleasant to the eyes, and a tree to be desired to make one wise, she took of the fruit thereof, and did eat, and gave also unto her husband with her; and he did eat.

Right at this time is when woman got it into her head she was equal to man, and much smarter than man, and that she should make the decisions. Go back to Genesis 2:18, "And the Lord God said, It is not good that the man to be alone; I will make him a help meet. This is to indicate that Adam is to be the leader, and Eve is to help him accomplish the things Adam was told by God to do. God first looked over the whole animal kingdom for a help meet for Adam, and there wasn't one available, because even though some of the beasts had the capability of working with Adam to be a help meet, they couldn't supply the companionship he needed.

In Genesis 2:21 and 22, God takes a rib from Adam and uses it to make Eve, and this isn't much different from cloning today. The fact that man has one less rib than a woman testifies to the truth of this verse. There has to be some speculation about how old were Adam and Eve at the time they were created? While there isn't any direct proof, it would seem realistic that they were young adults, perhaps in their late teens, around the time when learning things start to become important, somewhere around college age today.

Adam was supposed to be the leader, and Eve the help mate, but instead, Adam let Eve con him into doing what God told him not to do, and this makes Adam guilty of not acting as a leader he should have, and Eve is made out to be pure dumb in letting Satan lead her into mischief, especially since she'd been told not to do it. What happened to Satan we already know, he was stripped of the ability to walk upright, and had to crawl along, dragging his belly on the ground, and somewhere, maybe through Satan's influence on man, the snake became the culprit instead of the dragon, or giant lizard.

In Genesis 3:16 we read, "Unto the woman he said, I will greatly multiply thy sorrow and thy conception; in sorrow thou shalt bring forth children; and thy desire shall be to thy husband, and he shall rule over thee. Ever since that time man has fought the constant battle of the sexes, where men are of one mind, and the woman of another, and the separation came from when Satan first induced Eve to disobey God, and fall victim to Satan's charm. It has never changed from that time, and it can be summed up like this. A woman seeks out a male she admires, likes, or even loves, and she gets him into frame of mind to marry her. Afterward, she launches a campaign to change him to what she believes she wants in the man, and usually the man obliges and changes to suit his wife, but then the wife is no longer happy with him because he is not the same as he was at the first. This is pretty near the absolute truth about marriages, and those men who do change to what the woman thinks she wants, is generally unhappy in the marriage because he cannot be himself, but be someone else, and the woman doesn't like the situation because it isn't at all what she thought it would be like. He can't and won't change back, and she can't stand him the way he is, so they are at a impasse.

The man is as foolish about himself as the woman is about him, because he is complete within himself, and that's why a man can exist apart from people with little effort, but the woman cannot. No woman can live in exile alone for any great time because she is not complete without a man at her side. It goes back to the fact of what Adam said of Eve, "This is now bone of my bones, and flesh of my flesh: she will be called Woman, because she was taken out of Man. The oneness is the man taking the woman to wed, and not the other way round, and it is because of what is said in Genesis 2:24, "Therefore shall a man leave his father and his mother, and shall cleave unto his wife: and they shall be one flesh. Man was complete in the day he was created, and Woman was taken out of man to be a help meet, and wife to the man. Her desire is to her husband, and that is why a woman is more tightly bound in marriage than a man. The man's completeness, and the woman's incompleteness is what the vast majority of people do not understand. Here is an analogy. Two boats are anchored close together, but only one has an engine. The one with the engine can tow the other boat quite easily, but the one without the engine would have a hard time towing the other, and it is the same in the man and woman relationship. The man has the strength and power which the woman doesn't have, so the man can tow the woman along as a help meet, but he can't rely on her doing the towing because she hasn't the engine for it.

The woman's movement of today demanding they be made equal to men under the law is laughable from the prospect that it is entirely out of character because she is part of man, and can never be anything else. There's another practical side to it and it is this. God the Father, God the Son, and God the Holy Ghost are all masculine gender, and the male human is endowed with a holiness that women do not fully enjoy. There is no provision for women to become active in the worship of God as ministers, priests, or even teachers. This is written in I Timothy

2:11 and 12, "Let the woman learn in silence with all subjection. But I suffer not a woman to teach, nor to usurp authority over the man, but to be in silence.

A large part of the calamity today is that men have surrendered to the woman of the house the right and the leadership of the marriage, family, and worship, and in doing so are in the same spot as Adam was when he listened to Eve instead of God. Women have the propensity to act emotionally, and men have the tendency to be more thoughtful about any given situation. A lot of myths have been put about how the woman is better suited to run things, but this is Satan's way of striking at God. Unfortunately, men have again played into Satan's hand's through the women, because they allow the woman in their life to dominate, instead of be being in subjection. This reversal of the roles, can only lead to further condemnation by God.

The sad thing is that most women do not believe they should be in subjection to their husbands or to God. This is because in their upbringing they are coaxed and urged to use their feminine wiles against men, and men are taught women are the ones to make the choices, typical to how the beasts of the field are separated as males and females.

There has been a law enacted to give equal rights to women in the market place, in industry, and in the home, but how can you legislate against what God says in the natural and normal pattern for men and women to have? Who is there that can negate what God has decreed? although each day man tries to do so with the help of Satan.

It comes down to simple things. We are told in the Holy Bible in Leviticus 19:28, "Ye shall not make any cuttings in your flesh for the dead, nor print any marks upon you: I am the Lord. The current fad of wearing piercing rings, and of being tattooed fall under this law, and the wanton disfigurement of the holy temple is a serious offense against God. It comes down to the truth that if God wanted you to have these things, he would have put holes there for the rings, or put the tattoos on you himself. These two things are leftovers of cults worshipping false gods, and should be avoided by Christians and other Godly people. Can it not be understood that God wishes people to remain as they are without man made adornment? Each person is holy, and need no enhancement of the body, for God knows us spiritually, and it is God the Father, and Christ the Son, and God the Holy Ghost whom we need to please.

For Adam's part, God talks to him in Genesis 3:17, "And unto Adam he said, Because thou hast hearkened unto the voice of your wife, and hast eaten of the tree, of which I commanded thee, saying, Thou shalt not eat of it: cursed is the ground for thy sake; in sorrow thou shalt eat of it all the days of thy life. Thorns also and thistles shall it bring forth to thee, and thou shalt eat of the herb of the field; In the sweat of they face shalt thou eat bread, till thou return unto the ground; for out of it wast thou taken: for dust thou art, and to dust shalt thou return.

There can be no mistake that Adam was supposed to have shown more leadership, and refused to accept the fruit Eve offered him, and then God could have rectified the problem more easily. As it was, Adam and Eve blew their shot at immortality in the physical sense, by listening to Satan, and we too today are again doing the same thing by turning a deaf ear toward God and Christ, and are dancing to the tune of Satan. Is there no end to the sinful ways of man?

In Psalm 8:4 and 5, is written, "What is man, that thou art mindful of him? and the son of man that thou visitest him? For thou hast made him a little lower than the angels, and hast crowned him with glory and honor. It is time for man to awaken to the fact that we're supposed to be God's children, instead of acting like spoiled brats of Satan. It started with

Adam and Eve, but it has grown to unmitigated proportions. How long will God suffer man to disobey, without destroying him out of existence. He nearly did in the days of Noah, and if it hadn't been for this one man, all life on earth would have been destroyed by God, and earth today would be no different from Mars or any other barren planet in the Universe.

Doesn't it seem reasonable that given a second chance by God through Noah, and a third chance by Christ that man should have learned by now that the Lord's patience is being tried to its limit? How often does man have to reminded they are the children of God, and are expected to behave in a manner of their heritage?

Two things come out of Adam's punishment. Man is to be a farmer, and man is to eat of the food he raises, vegetation, and bread. Science is finding out today that man does better on the natural products of earth, the vegetable and fruits, the milk and honey, and the hard work it takes to produce these things to eat. The act of eating meat, which isn't part of the metabolism of man, didn't come about until after the flood of Noah's time, with the exception that perhaps the primitives ate meat, because they were hunters and gatherers. Adam was a farmer from the first day, so farming is God's choice of occupation for man. Here's why.

A person working in the field to produce enough food for his family has time to commune with God, and has a respect for the nature of the world, and if farming practices of Exodus and Leviticus were followed, the land would provide each family with a healthful living. To most this sounds like it would be a survival mode, but it wouldn't have to be. One of the worst things the world has done is go from being a farm community emphasis to an industry emphasis.

There is this question to be answered, and Christ asks it in Matthew 16:26, "For what is a man profited, if he shall gain the whole world and lose his own soul? or what shall a man give in exchange for his soul? Consider for a moment when man and animal worked the fields together to support the family, the wives and daughters put up the food for the winter, and the sons worked with the father. This meets the criteria God set for man and the family, because in this setting, every family member must contribute to the family fortune, and the family thereby is bound together by single minded purpose, serving God and family.

* * *

Today's farms are no longer God or family-oriented, but money or mammon-oriented, and this is an offense to God. The land is being drained of its ability to produce because more is taken out of it than can be replaced. The natural fertilizer of the farm animals put back naturally some of the nutrients and bacteria needed for a good harvest, and while commercial chemicals can replace the chemicals withdrawn by the harvest, they cannot put back the enzymes and bacteria the soil was depleted of by the harvest.

A man hoeing or otherwise working the fields manually has to rest from time to time, and in that moment he is refreshing himself, he has a moment to interact with God spiritually. The setting of driving in an air conditioned tractor listening to the radio while tilling the fields, offers little chance to communicate with God in the fashion he has set forth. He isn't impressed with the way man is treating the planet, and he no longer visits man who no longer has time for communing with God.

After they had disobeyed God's commandment about eating of the tree of knowledge, and becoming carnally minded, instead of spiritually minded, God realized there was no longer a need to separate this man and woman from the primitives living in the world. We read this in Genesis 3:23, "Therefore the Lord God sent him forth from the garden of Eden to till the soil from whence he was taken.

It's important to note that Adam returned to the land from which he was taken, and though this is still present in some people today, it has been overlooked by man throughout the ages. Adam had the minerals and the chemicals in a specific piece of ground, and this was a bond with him to the land. This is shown in animals or a particular region. Reindeer would be better off if they moved all the way south to live at the equator in lushness instead of the barren north, but their tie chemically, and through the ages has bound them to the north land. It is noticeable also in that as a species spread, it isn't in leaps and bounds, but as an increasing slow creeping, first one or two animals in search of new territory, and their offspring settling nearby, and so forth. The new range of land may take years to be settled by the population.

In the early years of man, the son's and daughters settled near their homes, and this provided a wealth of benefits. The families could interchange food and clothing, men could work together on projects needing more than one person, women could communicate and interact with the wives and children of the other family members, and the elderly could be assisted, honored and revered in their old age as declared to be right by God.

No such opportunity is afforded families living in the urban life style of today, and the loss of this vital element out of the lives of people is beginning to tell as people grow more socially cold, and aloof from the problems of other family members, especially the old. No one has the time or wishes to expend the effort to care for the old and feeble in the home, and relieve themselves of the burden by placing the elderly into nursing homes, and other retirement facilities.

Where it was once and honorable thing to look forward to the day when the parents retired from strenuous work to spend their last days contemplating their lives and their relationship with God and family, and interact with the grand children, it is no longer fashionable to do so. The elderly are expected by the younger generation to surrender their gained wealth as an inheritance to them, but they do not wish to be burdened by the elderly's presence. This separation was the all important link between man and God, for as we treat our parents, so do we treat our Father, God himself, and wanting his blessings and wealth, but little else.

Man had as a link to God, an earth connection that comes from being taken from the earth, and the home place on earth may have a chemical or magnetic attraction to man, the same way as birds and other animals have magnetic homing device. There is the old saying, and proven quite true, "You can take the boy from the mountains, but you can never take the mountains from the boy.

Adam and Eve then settled on the land from which Adam was created, and two sons were born to them, Able and Cain. Cain was a farmer and Able raised sheep, and at some time, Cain slew Able, and then gave the famous saying in Genesis 4:9, "And the Lord said unto Cain, Where is Abel thy brother? And he said, I know not: Am I my brother's keeper? This was the first murder in the family of the Caucasian race, and as far as can be determined, it was the first lie uttered to God by anyone in Adam's family. That means Cain got a double shot in history, one of being a liar, and one of being a murderer. God in punishment to Cain, cursed the earth that it would no longer yield its maximum to man, and he made Cain a vagabond, and thirdly he set a mark upon Cain. While there is no way to determine what this mark was, it would seem that it was probably a scar of some kind, visible to all who saw Cain, lest anyone kill him.

Now Cain had to go out, and he drifted around the garden of Eden to the east side, and settled in the land of Nod. The land of Nod was where the Mongoloids were located, and the Negroids were in Ethiopia, so when Cain took a wife, she had to be of Mongolian race of people.

From the Scripture of Genesis 4:17, "And Cain knew his wife; and she conceived and bare Enoch: and he builded a city, and called the name of the city after the name of his son, Enoch. The Mongoloids were the primitive people brought to earth by Lucifer, and there wasn't any guarantee that Cain could father a child with his wife because they were of different beginning, so it is mentioned that she did conceive, and produced a child, and Enoch is important in the history of man because he is the first child born having the blood of two major races within him, and he is the first child of the Mongolian race to have the Spirit of God in him, through his father, Cain. This sets the pattern of how God is going to integrate all mankind into being the children of God. As the sons of Adam and Eve marry into the primitive races, and have offspring, the offspring become children of God, having the Spirit of God passed to them through their father.

From the verse, it has to mean that Cain was the leader in the area, because he built a city, and called it after the name of his son, Enoch. This has to mean the primitives looked up to Cain and to his leadership, evidently because Cain had better mental capacities than did the primitives. They could work with metal and stone, but Cain knew how to use these materials to build with, and it could be suspected that when they built the city, the whole tribe settled down to living in one place. That places the city somewhere toward Mount Ararat, and it's reasonable to believe they slowly migrated toward Asia.

Adam and Eve had another son, named Seth and from Seth came Enos, and from Enos came Cainan, and from Cainan came Mahalaleel, and from Mahalaleel came Jared, and from Jared came Enoch, and from Enoch came Methuselah, and from Methuselah came Lamech and from Lamech came Noah.

115

This is the straight line of descendants from Adam and Eve to Noah, and the wife of Noah was also descended from Adam and Eve, because God wanted the line of descendants of the coming Hebrews to be pure. Noah and his wife had three sons, Ham, Shem, and Japheth.

In Genesis 6: 1, we read, "And it came to pass, when men began to multiply on the face of the earth, and daughters were born unto them, That the sons of God saw the daughters of men that they were fair; and they took them wives of all which they chose. All three races were expanding, but the male offspring of Adam and Eve, referred to as the sons of God, saw the mixed blooded females were two things. They were fair of skin as in the Eurasian and the Mulatto, and they were beautiful women in features, and they took all the wives they wanted, which was the beginning of polygamy. It has to be noted that it is doubtful the pure races in the primitives had such a custom of more than one wife, because it wasn't possible for a man to feed, clothe, and house very many people on a hunt and gather life style, but the descendants of Adam and Eve were farmers, and wealthy by the standards of the other races, well able to support more than one wife and several broods of children.

In Genesis 6:4, is written, "There were giants in those days and also after that, when the son's of God came in unto the daughters of men, and they bare children to them, the same became mighty men which were of old, men of renown. When the male descendants of Adam and Eve took these wives of mixed breeds, the male offspring were huge in comparison to their parents, and this was the throw back to the primitive people. The primitive people were evidently much bigger people than were the newly arrived Caucasians, but as they intermixed, the people grew smaller in stature by the action of genetics. At this time on earth there were these combinations. Caucasians with Caucasians, Negroid with Negroid, and Mongoloid with Mongoloid, then there was Caucasian with

Negroid, and Caucasian with Mongoloid, and the Mongoloid with Negroid, and then the intermixing of the mixed bloods of these, with the three pure races, and other mixed bloods, so it was a hodgepodge assortment of people on earth at this time. When these huge men came into the world as giants, probably like some today's football and basketball heroes standing seven feet tall and weighing up to 300 pounds, they were compared to the people standing five foot two or so, and weighing 140 to 160 pounds, seemingly a giant. These men were well known, because they were the champions of the tribe they lived in, able to handle several ordinary men with apparent ease.

Goliath, whom David slew was such a person, and as pointed out, today there are many such people in the world, and this testifies back to the times the races were intermixed, and these giant people came about.

There came a time when God looked at man on earth and he didn't like what he saw, so in Genesis 6:6 is recorded, "And it repented the Lord that he had made man on the earth, and it grieved him at his heart. Think of it. The wickedness of those days is nothing compared to the wickedness and evil in man today, and it's completely foolish to think God is going to let this evil go on. In Genesis 6:7, "And the Lord said, I will destroy man whom I have created from the face of the earth; both man, and beast, and the creeping thing, and the fowls of the air; for it repenteth me that I have made them. Read that over again and let it sink in as to how close God was to destroying everything he had created, and went back to having only the heaven Universe, with the angels serving him! Can it be imagined how dumb all mankind has become, not to recognize the inherent danger of constantly flaunting his wickedness before God?

If it hadn't been for one man being God's ideal of man, the whole creation would have been destroyed, and there would be no such thing as the Universe, earth, and man. Noah found grace in the eyes of the Lord, and God made a covenant with Noah, and it is written in Genesis 6:18, "But with thee will I establish my covenant; and thou shalt come into the ark, thou, and thy sons, and thy wife, and thy son's wives with thee. Out of the whole world of the primitives, and of the mixed people, and of the descendants of Adam and Eve only eight people would remain alive after the flood. Two things have to be evident. There are three major races of people on earth today, and they had to be preserved through Noah's sons. Noah, his wife, and his sons were from Adam and Eve, and that means one of the son's wives had to be Negroid, one Mongoloid, and the other Caucasian. Prior to the flood there were a mixture of the three pure races, and mixtures of blood in between them, but after the flood, from the sons there were no children born that did not have the Spirit of God in them, and that means God had accomplished bringing all the primitives into the family of God's children, and Lucifer's attempt to outwit God was foiled.

Probably the most asked question about this period of time is whether or not a global flood did occur? Several bits of information go together to prove that it did happen. Science agrees there was a global flood, by a flood layer being found throughout the world. By scripture in Genesis 7:19 and 20, we get the depth of the water. "And the waters prevailed exceedingly upon the earth; and all the high hills, that were under the whole heaven were covered. Fifteen cubits upward did the waters prevail; and the mountains were covered. It is known by Scripture in Genesis 8:4, "And the ark rested in the seventh month, on the seventeenth day of the month, upon the mountains of Ararat.

Mount Ararat is located on the Armenian plateau, and culminates in two peaks with the highest almost 17,000 feet high. Considering the mountains were under water, and the mention of fifteen cubits means the top of the highest peak was covered with about 23 feet of water, a cubit is equal to about eighteen inches. This means the entire earth was under water except for the highest mountain peaks on earth the Alps, but they could not be seen from that vantage point, and we aren't sure the Alps were that high in those days. It can be said for sure that places like Mount Rainier, in Washington state, and the other taller mountains on North and South America were all under water. Even if the highest peaks of the Alps were not covered, they were at a high altitude and of solid rock without any ability to sustain any type life. It is then fairly certain that all life on the planet save for that aboard the ark was destroyed in the flood.

The flood lasted 150 days, which ensured the total destruction of life, and then the waters began to abate. It is known, that if all the water in the atmosphere were to come back to earth, and the ice at the poles of the planet melted, the planet would once again be covered by water. This means the flood engineered by God was probably induced by sudden change in climate. In recent years scientists have become aware of the El Nino, and El Nina effect, where either cold water or warm water moves northward, or southward, and makes dramatic weather changes world wide. This makes the flood entirely reasonable in light of the severe local flooding during the rapid weather changes effected by the warm and cold water movement.

During WWII, pilots flying over Mount Ararat, reported seeing some type of ship parked on the steep slopes of the highest peak of Ararat, and took pictures of the craft. From the reports given by the pilots, and the photos, it was determined that the dimensions and looks of the craft were the same as the profile of Noah's ark in the Holy Bible. A ground party of scientists was launched to investigate the ship, but because of the war, the scientists were denied access to the mountain. The ship slid steadily down the slopes of the mountain, and after the war, another ground party of investigators was hurriedly launched to find the ship. They arrived to get a few pictures of it close up, and a piece or two of the wood from the ark, but then weather set in, and the expedition had to abandon their study. The ship disappeared that winter into a deep crevasse, and will probably never be seen again.

Working with the photos, and the measurements of the ark in the Holy Bible, scientists and engineers built a scale model of the ark, and were surprised to find the craft could endure any weather that might have been present during the flood. It was a very stable craft, water tight under the most extreme conditions, and for years, scientists marveled at the technology used in the craft at such a early time in man's history.

In Genesis 9:1 is recorded, "And God blessed Noah and his sons, and said unto them, Be fruitful, and multiply, and replenish the earth. H ere again God uses the word replenish rather than fill, and this supports the concept that Adam and Eve were directed by God to replenish or replace the primitives on earth at the time, and now Ham, Shem, and Japheth are to replenish earth with people, but with the exception that all races will now be classified as man, because they all have the Spirit of God in them, and the physical body of every man is now the temple of God.

With the inclusion of all mankind into being the children of God, each person regardless of race, is required to pay homage to God, and to follow his ways. This fulfills what is written in Isaiah 45:23, "I have sworn by myself, the word is gone out of my mouth in righteousness, and shall not return, That unto me every knee shall bow, every tongue shall swear.

Prior to the flood, everything on earth was a herbivore, and lived together in harmony, with each creature filling a niche in the scheme of nature. Now, God changes the picture, by what is written starting in Genesis 9:2, "And the fear of you and the dread of you shall be upon every beast of the earth, and upon every fowl of the air, upon all that moveth upon the earth, and upon all the fishes of the sea; into your hand they are delivered. Every moving thing that liveth shall be meat for you: even as the green herb have I given you all things. But flesh with the life thereof, which is the blood thereof, shall ye not eat. And surely your blood of your lives will I require; at the hand of every beast will I require it, and at the hand of man; at the hand of every man's brother will I require the life of man. Whoso sheddeth man's blood, by man shall his blood be shed: for in the image of God made he man.

It is interesting to note that this commandment okays killing the animals of the world for food, (not sport), and states clearly that a person wantonly killing another person will be killed for his sin against God, because the physical body, the temple of God is being defiled. Most do not understand that all sin is committed against God, and not against man, because man is the property of God, the same as the earth and the Universe are the properties of God. We are therefore unable to forgive an act by a fellow man, because the sin is against God, and only God can forgive a sin against him. We may bear the brunt of the sin, but this is in the same light as when someone damages your car in an accident. The car doesn't receive payment for the damage done to it, but as the owner you are paid. While man may be damaged by another person, God is the collector of the repayment as the owner of man.

In Genesis 10:5 is written, "By these were the isles of the Gentiles divided in their lands; everyone after his tongue, after their families, in their nations. The word Gentiles actually means those who are not Jews or Christians, and in this text it must mean those of Mongoloid or Asian descent. Japheth and his sons then went west from Ararat to places like Ankara, and toward the ancient city Troy.

Ham and his sons settled along the coast of the Mediterranean sea and founded the cities of Sodom and Gomorrah, and the descendants of Shem and Japheth intermixed to bring new nations into existence, It has to be concluded that Ham's wife was of the Negroid race, and Japheth's wife was of the Mongoloid race, and that means the Caucasian race came from Shem and we see this to be true because Abraham was a direct descendant of Shem. From the Scriptures, it can be determined, that while Japheth and Ham's families mixed, Shem's families remained a pure Caucasian race. This evidently was done by God to preserve the line of Adam and Eve. In the modern day, the heritage of the Jews can be traced back from this generation to Adam and Eve. It could then be said that Adam and Eve were the first Jews.

There came a time, when the people got together and decided to build a tower that would reach to heaven, and they were going to give themselves a name that would never be forgotten, and must be where the names of the nations came into reality, so each nation was associated with a particular family. Hams descendants populated the lands to the south, hence the Egyptian, which came from the mixed bloods between Hams descendants, and Japheth's descendants, and to include Ethiopia, which was established as the nation of the Negroid. It wasn't until God changed the language, and isolated the people into different nations, and cultures, that races once more became a dominating factor. The Ethiopians became the modern day Negroid race, the Asians the Mongoloid race, and the Jews the Caucasian race. Peoples like the Egyptians having mixed blood became their own minor race, as American Indian, the South American Indian, and the natives of the south sea islands. This is obvious by the Mexican people who are a mixture of the mixed race of Indians and the Spanish, which is also a mixed race.

Since the time of the tower of Babel, man has tried to overcome the barriers put between them by God so they would not be a single people, but a diverse people, with different languages, customs, and understandings. The only common connection between the nations that should be in place today should be the belief in God, and the acceptance that each is here to serve God. In doing this, the nation is best served by understanding that God does not take the making of war between people as a light thing, but as a punishment to those who refuse to honor and worship him. However, it has to be remembered the greatest force on earth that is developing is secularism, or atheism, and that is under the leadership of Satan, and against God. Those nations becoming affiliated with the nations under Satan's control are just creeping into the news of today, and the nations starting to fall to Satan's army is becoming more pronounced each day in the news. Add into that mix the nations which believe they are serving God, and are not, and you have the making of the calamity which is to come upon the earth in the not too distant future.

The world today is struggling toward the New World Order, a single government for the world, a single currency, a single system of weights and measures, and a single religion or belief. The new tower of Babel is the joint effort of nations putting together the space station, and this new tower of Babel is hoped to bring back the unity to being one people world wide. There's only one thing wrong in that thinking. It violates what God wants people and the world of man to do. God knows the world of man is headed for enslavement to Satan, and how far he will let us go down this road is anybody's guess. But for those who are interested, read about the end time.

Out of Shem came the people who lived around the ancient town of Ur, which is some north of the land they now own. Shem's descendants went down to Terah, who had three sons, Abram, Nahor, and Haran. Haran died, but he left Lot his son. Nahor married Milcah, the daughter of Haran, and Nahor and Milcah had a daughter they named Mileah, and a son they named Iscah. There's nothing said about where Sarai, Abram's wife was from, but it had to be from among kin folk.

Terah then took Abram and Sarai, and Lot and his wife, and they left Ur and drifted down to the land of Caanan, and there was apparently a city named Haran where they lived, and there Terah, the father of Abram, died.

In Genesis 12:1 we read about Abram's calling. "Now the Lord had said unto Abram, Get thee out of thy country, and from thy kindred, and from thy father's house, unto a land that I will shew thee. This is the first pr omise of God concerning ownership of any land on the planet, and it is made exclusively to Abram. Here's what God told Abram in Genesis 12:2 and 3, "And I will make of thee a great nation, and I will bless thee, and make thy name great; and thou shalt be a blessing. That is the first establishment of a favored nation status in existence. In Genesis 12:6 and 7 is recorded, "And Abram passed through the land unto the place of Sichem, unto the plain of Moreh. And the Canaanite was then in the land. And the Lord appeared unto Abram, and said, Unto thy seed will I give this land: and there he builded and altar unto the Lord, who appeared before him. God has now set things up to bring the Jews into being, and they are to own the land God gave to Abram's seed. This was to be the chosen line of God, the Hebrew nation, but at the time he talked with Abram, he wasn't talking about Abram owning the land, but Abram's and Sarai's offspring.

Abram lived in Canaan, and God came to him. Genesis 13:14, "And the Lord said unto Abram, after that Lot was separated from him, Lift up now thine eyes, and look from the place where thou art northward, and southward, and eastward and westward: for all the land which thou seest, to thee will I give it, and to thy seed for ever. And I will make thy seed as the dust of the earth: so that if a man can number the dust of the earth, then shall thy seed also be numbered. Arise, walk through the land in the length and breadth of it; for I will give it unto thee. This is the second time God has told Abraham he and his seed is to possess the land called Israel today.

Sarai was barren, and she had an Egyptian hand maid, and Sarai said to Abram, "Behold now, the Lord hath restrained me from bearing: I pray thee go in unto my maid; it may be that I may obtain children by her. And Abram hearkened unto the voice of Sarai. This is the first case of a surrogate mother on record, and like most times, when women talk men into doing things they shouldn't, it back fired. We have Eve talking Adam into eating of the forbidden fruit, and now Abram heeding the word of his wife, and marrying a second wife, which was against God's word, and having a son by her called Ishmael. When this happened, Genesis 16:5 occurred, "And Sarai said unto Abram, My wrong be upon thee: I have given my maid into thy bosom; and when she saw she had conceived, I was despised in her eyes: the Lord judge between me and thee.

Abraham told Sarai that Hagar was her maid, and she could do with her as she wished, and Sarai dealt harshly with Hagar, and Hagar ran away. An angel told her to return to Sarai, and in Genesis 16: 10 is recorded, "And the angel of the Lord said unto her, I will multiply thy seed exceedingly, that it shall not be numbered for the multitude. And the angel of the Lord said unto her. Behold thou art with child, and shalt bear a son, and thou shalt call his name Ishmael; because the Lord hath heard thy affliction. And he will be a wild man; his hand will be against every man, and every man's hand against him; and he shall dwell in the place of all his brethren. The Arab na tions of the world are these descendants of Ishmael.

When Abram was old in Genesis 17: 1, we read, "And when Abram was ninety years old and nine the Lord appeared unto Abram, and said unto him, I am, the Almighty God; walk before me, and be thou perfect. And I will make my covenant between me and thee, and will multiply thee exceedingly. And Abram fell on his face : and God talked with him saying, As for me, behold, my covenant is with thee, and thou shalt be a father of many nations. Neither shall thy name be anymore called

Abram, but thy name shall be Abraham: for the father of many nations have I made thee. And I will make thee exceedingly fruitful, and I will make nations of thee, and kings shall come out of thee. And I will establish my covenant between me and thee and thy seed after thee in their generations for an everlasting covenant, to be a God unto thee and to thy seed after thee. And I will give unto thee, and to thy seed after thee, the land wherein thou art a stranger, all the land of Canaan, for an everlasting possession; and I will be their God. In the covenant, all Abraham's offspring and all the people he ruled over, had to be circumcised. So as it stands, the Jews who still are circumcised own all of the land Israel now occupies. As long as the Jews keep their part of the covenant, they own the land they have.

Even though Sarah was way over age for conceiving, she did conceive and bring forth a Son called Isaac. God had told Abraham that he was to send for a wife, from his own kindred for Isaac, but that he was not to marry with a Canaanite woman, and Abraham sent a servant to where his brother Nahor still lived, and the servant returned with Rebekeh, the daughter of Milcah and Nahor.

In Genesis 25:23 is recorded, "And the Lord God said unto her Two nations are in thy womb, and two manner of people shall be separated from thy bowels; and the one people shall be stronger than the other people: and the elder shall serve the younger.

Esau was hairy and red, and Jacob was a plain child. Esau became a hunter, and Jacob a farmer. One day Esau returned from hunting. Here's what's recorded in Genesis 25:30, "And Esau said to Jacob, Feed me, I pray thee, with that red pottage; for I am faint: there fore his name was called Edom. And Jacob said, Sell me this day your birthright. And Esau said, Behold I am at the point to die: and what profit shall this birthright be to me?

Esau then swore away his birthright to Jacob. These eventually wound up being the two nations Judah and Israel.

The history of man today is enshrouded in the Holy Bible, and few have ever taken the time to reason it out to any conclusion, let alone the right conclusion, but preferring to let others decide what it all means. In essence, seeing the covenant made with Abraham and his seed seems to indicate that only the Jews are to be honored as the children of God, but that isn't the case, and it in the acceptance of Christ as the Savior that we find all believers are elevated to that status.

CHAPTER 5

The Savior

Never in the history of the world has any man left such a mark as the man called Jesus. The very mark of the years of time is based on his arrival on earth, and his departure on earth, though he only spent about thirty three years with man. The man called Jesus, through modem day teaching, has been altered way out of character by man from what he really was like, so there remains little resemblance of the real God left to understand.

Christ is depicted as a meek, gentle person who wouldn't hurt a fly, full of compassion and understanding, and a person who loved all men. Whoever dreamed up this description of Christ has never taken the time to look closely at the Savior, nor have they tried to understand what Christ was all about. The biggest misunderstanding is that today's preachers teach about this messenger, but they don't teach the message Christ brought to man. When is it ever spoken of in any church, about the new government that is to come upon earth, which is to be brought here by Christ, and being one that will last for a thousand years under Christ's rule? And then after that time, there is to be another judgment, with only the worthy going on to live with God the Father, God the Son, and God the Holy Ghost in immortal status, as the true children of God. What is preached, is how Christ was a benevolent person, dying for man's sin, so all could go to heaven. This is a terrible distortion in belief, for it is false teaching, and the reason it is false is because man has seen fit to ignore the message the Savior brought. It is not that Christ didn't die for man's sin, but what good is that dying if man is lost again by the ignorance of his own ways? Can it be imagined for a moment, that if Christ entered into a church today unrecognized, in many churches he would be asked not to partake of communion by the church officials, because they could not ascertain his worthiness to take communion? They cite what is written in I Corinthians 11: 27, "Wherefore whosoever shall eat of this bread, and drink of this cup of the Lord unworthily shall be guilty of the body and blood of the Lord. Then in I Corinthians "For he that eateth, and drinketh unworthily, eateth, and drinketh damnation to himself, not discerning the Lord's body. These two verses are cited as reason to have closed communion, and this severs the common bond held between all Christians, and between all men. The reason why this should not be subjected to enforcement by the church officials is written in I Corinthians 11:28, "But let a man examine himself, and so let him eat of that bread, and drink of that cup.

Who on earth is worthy to eat of the body and blood of Christ? If the truth be known, none on earth would be worthy, for we have not come to understand Christ's ways or message, but are locked into the smothering ignorance of man's interpretation of the Word.

What of the millions who do not recognize Christ as the Savior of man, but await the Savior? The Truth has come and gone, and many men have missed the boat so to say. Except they be converted to Christ, they shall be judged upon their works, for the Saving Grace has come and gone, and under this judgment few will be saved. Of the twelve tribes of the Jews, only 144,000, will be lifted up, and of the Jews that have lived, it is few in comparison. Of the Islamic there is no mention, and it will be that all must be judged upon their works, because of their disbelief in Jesus. The promise to Hagar and to Ishmael has been fulfilled, and the wildness of the nations from Ishmael's seed, now should amend to mutual understanding that Christ awaits their conversion.

Howbeit the world will wait until the end time is upon them, and they see Christ coming with his angels in the clouds, that then they will believe and groan in agony, knowing they will be found unfit and unworthy of life in Christ's kingdom?

Of the eastern religions, and of the cults, and of the false religions, it is time to cast off the untruth for the truth of God, and understand that Christ is king, both in heaven and on earth. Though his throne on earth be empty for a while longer, the day will shortly come, when Satan shall be cast out, and Christ seated as the head of the government. All mankind should recognize, and convert before this time, if they are to enjoy the presence and fruits of Christ.

Were it not for the Savior, all would be condemned to destruction, even as the world of Noah's time was condemned to destruction for their wickedness. God is again approaching the time when he repents having made the Universe, the earth, and man, and except for those who are safely bound to Christ, there shall none be saved. Is this a harsh rendering by God? Who has ever encouraged weeds to grow in their lawn? It is the same with God, why let the wicked flourish in his kingdom?

Imagine for a moment the expectation the Jews have for the Savior, they expect a strong leader, one who can vanquish the enemies they have on every hand, and this is the primary reason Jesus was never accepted by the Jews as being the Christ. The leaders in the Jewish faith of that day, and the leaders of the Jewish faith of this day, are of the same contention, and wait for a Messiah who has come and gone, and soon to return again without their ever recognizing him. Their blindness is wrapped up in their traditions and their stiff necked refusal to honor God the Son, and this yoke of hardship is not to be broken until the end time. Only then will the realization come, that they were stiff necked and unbelieving, a serious sin against God. What made Jesus the Christ so special is recorded in the Holy Bible for all to read and understand. Enough highlights of his life will be given for a person to get the general gist of his testimony, how to get to become the children of God.

The general flavor is Jesus, being the Son of God, on earth, and in the flesh, to testify that of all men which has or ever will walk the earth, it is only he that will inherit all things of the Father. The role of leadership in the world of man was turned over to the Son, when Christ was of age to began his ministry, and his earthly reign extended for twenty years, at which time he surrendered himself as the final blood sacrifice for the atonement of man's sins against God. Never has such a world wide change been effected in the world as wrought by the birth and death of Jesus Christ.

The change was not only evident in the world, but also in heaven, and this need be looked at carefully to gain its importance to mankind. Here is the prediction of his birth by Isaiah five hundred years before his birth. It is written in Isaiah 9:6, "For unto us a child is born, unto us a son is given: and the government shall be upon his shoulder: and his name shall be called Wonderful, Councellor, the mighty God, The everlasting Father, the Prince of Peace. This prediction was misconstrued by the Jews to believe the coming Messiah was going to be a strong political leader, a king that would vanquish their many enemies, and give them everlasting peace. This was the prophecy that caused the Jews to continue to wait for the Messiah, and are still waiting today, two thousand years after Christ left earth.

The events in heaven just before the birth of Jesus on earth, is described in Revelation 12:1 through 6, "And there appeared a great wonder in heaven; a woman clothed with the sun, and the moon under her feet, and upon her head a crown of twelve stars. This is the virgin Mary, bearing the glory of God's light around her, and raised spiritually to heaven, to look down on the moon. On her head is the crown of Israel, meaning she represents the Jews by the crown, and the twelve stars are the twelve tribes of Israel. This in itself should be enough for Israel to recognize that as the prophecy of Isaiah says, the Messiah will be born of the Jews, and will rule the twelve tribes.

Then in Revelation 12:2, "And she being with child cried, travailing in birth, and pained to be delivered. This is the conception of Mary, and her readiness to give birth, and this is tied to Matthew 1:23, "Behold a virgin shall be with child, and shall bring forth a son, and they shall call his name Emmanuel, which being interpreted is, God with us. Since the child was named Jesus, it must be accepted this is to mean Emmanuel, or God with us. Prior to this time, the name Jesus had never been used, but is a common name today, especially in the Latino community of men.

In Revelation 12:3 is written, "And there appeared another wonder in heaven; and behold, a great red dragon, having seven heads and ten horns, and seven crowns upon his heads. This is the power structure in the world at that time, the Roman empire with the different nations and allies ruling that part of the earth in those days, and under the leadership of Satan, now pledged to being the adversary to God.

Satan knew, after the flood, when all men now had the Spirit of God within them, that his kingdom on earth had been destroyed by God, and had been taken over by God to be included in God's kingdom. As he stands in heaven, watching God prepare to send his own son down to earth as the final blood sacrifice in atonement of man's sins, Satan gathers in a full third of the God's angels, and sends them to earth; and he leads them in an attempt to destroy man's Savior as soon as he is born, and he attempts this through Herod the king. Herod tried to get the information about Christ's birth from the wise men seeking Christ, but upon leaving Herod headed for Bethlehem, a star rose in the east and traveled before them until it stood over where the young child lay. There they brought unto him their gifts, and worshipped him and then left going back to their own country using another way so they wouldn't have to report to Herod where the child was to be found.

Here's what to consider. Satan wanted to prevent man from having a Savior, because he was adept at wresting men away from God, and without a Savior, most men could be converted to worshipping him instead of God. In this he'd have his own kingdom, and could rival God as being the Highest power.

Satan worked through Herod who didn't want to surrender his kingship over the Jews to this prophesied king of the Jews, and with this in mind, and having failed to locate Jesus through the wise men, he took other steps, and we read of it in Matthew 2:16. "Then Herod when he saw that he was mocked of by the wise men, was exceedingly wroth, and sent forth, and slew all the children that were in Bethlehem, and in all the coasts thereof, from two years old and under, according to the time which he had diligently enquired of the wise men.

We return back to Revelation 12:5, "And she brought forth a man child who was to rule all the nations with a rod of iron: and the child was caught up unto God and his throne. There is a plural meaning in this, and it is this. Christ's first trip on earth was to fulfill the prophecy that a Messiah or Savior would come to the Jews, and the second is that through Christ's teaching, and the selecting of the first disciples he was setting up the structure of his government on earth. This government isn't complete today, because man is drifting away from the Christian ethics and structure, but it will be completed when Christ returns in the not too distant future.

The promise from God to the Jews was for a Messiah and a leader, and that promise has been partially fulfilled by Jesus being born into the Jewish nations and is to be king of the twelve tribes. This need be explored a little deeper, because what there is of Israel today is not representative of the entire twelve tribes of the Jews. The power, the strength, the prosperity of the twelve tribes of Israel lies in the Christian nations of the world, and this is borne out by the United States of America, Canada, Australia, and the commonwealth of England, and most of the predominantly Caucasian nations. The deceit is in the nations that have already turned their back on God, and are siding with Satan, and these are the nations under the leadership of Germany. There are two major opposing forces taking shape in the world today, and it is these. The re-establishment of the Roman empire of Christ's day, and this is in evidence by the religious leader of Rome, the Pope, moving toward trying to establish some type of inroads into the nation of Israel today, and at the same time, catering to the fourth Reich, or power rising in Germany today.

The rhetoric that religions should blend together is only rhetoric to entrap the unwary, and further the establishment of the Roman empire, wherein Catholicism would play a major role as the religion of the world. But in this, the Pope has become the ploy of the atheist government that is going to come about on earth with Germany as the leader.

This is why Christ, in his ministry, preached about the coming kingdom of God, and preached that only in that time would the nations become united under a single government where peace and prosperity would reign throughout the whole earth.

Man is trying to return to the tower of Babel, to one language, one government (name) and one belief and all these are wrong goals for mankind to undertake. When God divided the people from Noah's sons upon the earth, and when they decided to build the tower of Babel, God changed the languages, and divided the people into different nations, and cultures, trying to get them to understand that the key to them becoming united into a single nation, and culture would not come until Christ returned to earth. The differences in cultures were supposed to keep the different people apart, to preserve that people in their race, religion, and culture until such time as

Christ returned to unite all men into a single unified nation, culture, and religion.

As is usual with Satan, he is there trying to thwart God and Christ's mission, and to enslave man unto himself, and he goes through a great deal of trouble to get what he wants, and as the gullibility of man increases as it has since the time of Christ, Satan will make more and more inroads into enslaving man.

The current attempt is the New World Order, wherein the world will come under one government, and that government is in the making in Europe today under the leadership of Germany.

Consider this for a moment. Germany is about two thirds the size of Texas and wields more power than many greater nations. From where does this power come? Germany has had three Reichs, or realms of power, which has caused two world wars and is now launching the fourth Reich, which is hoped to put the rule of earth under German control. Is not this the same goal Germany had set before it in the prior Reichs? The master race syndrome is far from removed from these people, and they are moving toward the time of the last war to be fought on planet earth, the battle of Armageddon, on the Megiddo plain. It is in the understanding that Germany is the tool used by Satan for this next assault on the world to enslave it.

When Satan didn't manage to kill the Savior when he was born, he went back to Heaven to make a try at God's throne there, and we read about it in Revelation 12:7 and 8, "And there was a war in heaven: Michael and his angels fought against the dragon; and the dragon fought, and his angels, And prevailed not; neither was their place found any more in heaven."

Satan was cast out of heaven along with his angels, and they are at work on earth today, deceiving individuals and nations into the wrong way of thinking, and that deceit comes about through using perceived truth rather than the absolute truth of the Holy Bible, God's word to man.

The first thing Satan did was to tempt Jesus, and he led Jesus up into the wilderness, where Jesus fasted forty days and forty nights. If this seems a bit far out it is because people have never had to endure such deprivation. Many flyers in WWII found themselves down at sea, and without rescue. Many survived for more than forty days drinking only rain water, unable to catch a fish, or snag a bird. The body of man is more resilient than a person would suppose, and we are encouraged by the Holy Bible, to fast often, and pray. The fasting before prayer seems to be an indication of how earnest we are in that which we ask God to do, and an action God recognizes as an earnest plea. Jesus explained this in Matthew 17:2 1, when the disciples could not cast out a devil from a man. Christ told them it was mostly because they didn't believe they could cast the devil out, but then added, "Howbeit this kind goeth not out but by prayer and fasting.

The habit of fasting and prayer does several things for a person. It sharpens the mind toward God, and it demonstrates the person is willing to deprive themselves for receiving God's favor. This has the effect of being similar to a sacrifice offered to God for success in a coming battle.

Satan tempted Christ by saying to him, if you're the Son of God, then command these stones be turned into bread, but Christ answered and told Satan that man didn't live by bread alone but by the words that came from God's mouth, and this a is a very important understanding for every person to have concerning their daily life. Whenever the woman, or whoever does the cooking in the family, asks the family what they would like to eat, so they can prepare the meal, it is a token of how prosperous God has made that family. As long as you have choice, there is prosperity, for in many parts of the world, and in many homes, there is no choice, and little prosperity.

Then Satan told Jesus to jump off the top of the temple, and the angels would bear him up, to which Christ replied, that a person should not tempt the Lord God. This should be warning enough to people not to take chances in doing the simple things in life like, speeding in their autos, taking drugs that you are unsure of, acting reckless with any piece of equipment, firearm, or knife, or anything such as acting smart on a snow mobile, or in a boat. Any of these things is the tempting of God, and you may get away with it once, maybe even twice, but the odds are, you will push God to the limit and he will respond, and let you kill yourself. That's not being very wise or smart.

Then Satan told Christ he'd give him world to rule if he'd fall down and worship Satan as a god, and Jesus told him to get away, because it was written, "Thou shalt worship the Lord thy God, and only him shalt thou serve.

This is one of the best pieces of advice that can be given all men, and people need to follow this advice. What good is it to worship and honor fellow man, material things, and false gods?

The next piece of sound advice is in Matthew 4:17, "From that time Jesus began to preach, and to say, Repent: for the kingdom of God is at hand. So many have become tired of hearing that God's kingdom is at hand, and fail to recognize the proof is in the history since Jesus preached it. Jesus himself fulfilled the promise of God to the Jews that a Messiah and a Savior was coming, though it took 500 years for it to happen after Isaiah told the Jews about the event.

Christ has been gone from the world two thousand years, and that in itself should be taken that his return is imminent, and in his telling of the signs to his disciples of when they could expect him to return, a study of those signs leads to the belief that we are about to enter that end time.

One of the biggest obstacles Jesus had was the opposition to him by the leaders of the Jewish religion, and that blockade is still in place. This has to be analyzed out, and what applies here to the Jews, applies also to the other established religions in the world. The primary objective of the leaders of the established religions on earth today is control of the people. This is seen quite clearly in the eastern religions with their masters, the Jewish religion with their Rabbis, in the Islamic by their religious and government rulers, and in the Christians by the denominational leaders. All these are interested not in service to the people as Christ was, to win each individual to his way, but in a broader sense of preaching how each individual should think and believe. These doctrines of man is exactly what Christ is talking about in Matthew 15:8 and 9, "This people draweth nigh unto me with their mouth, and honoreth me with their lips: but their heart is far from me. But in vain do they worship me, teaching for doctrines the commandments of men. These are the people who have been taught all the wrong things about Christ and the Christian movement in the world. They have turned the word of God and Christ toward their own belief, for their own worldly enhancement and glory, forgetting what the original treatise of Christ in the Christian movement. It is written in Matthew 5:19, "Whosoever therefore shall break one of these least commandments, and shall teach men so, he shall be called the least in the kingdom of heaven: but whosoever shall do and teach them, the same shall be called great in heaven. What happens to these tea chers and people? The answer is in Matthew 15:14, "Leave them alone: they be blind leaders of the blind. And if the blind lead the blind, both shall fall into the ditch.

These churches are the same that teach that Jesus did away with the law of Moses, and that the ten commandments have been superseded by grace or indulgence by Christ, and this simply isn't the truth. Here's how Christ addressed this question of the law it is in Matthew 5:17 and 18, "Think not that I am come to destroy the law, or the prophets: I am not come to destroy, but to fulfill. For verily I say unto you, Till heaven and earth pass, one jot or tittle shall in no wise pass from the law, till all be fulfilled. What Christ preached was the amplification of the commandments and law. He gives as an example in Matthew 5:21 and 22, how we should accept and abide in the law. "Ye have heard it was said by them of old time, Thou shalt not kill: and whosoever shall kill shall be in danger of the judgment. But I say unto you, That whosoever is angry with his brother without a cause shall be in danger of the judgment: and whosoever shall say to his brother, Raca, shall be in danger of the council: but whosoever shall say Thou fool shall be in danger of hell fire. This didn't remove the penalty for killing another person, but clarified that you are in danger even for unrighteous anger or declares hatred for his brother, or if he calls his brother a fool is in deep trouble!

He does the same in Matthew 5:27 and 28 concerning adultery and lust. "Ye have heard that it was said of them of old time, Thou shalt not commit adultery: But I say unto you, That whosoever looketh at a woman to lust after her hath committed adultery with her already in his heart. This means that man's way of looking at this in saying, "It's okay to look and think but don't touch, is wrong in the eyes of Christ and God. These are only a couple of examples of where man has gone wrong in his thinking concerning God, Christ, and the judgment. Christ has told you that he did not come to change the law, then why believe you are exempt from God's laws and commandments? The confusion seems to be in Christ serving as the final blood sacrifice for the sins of man. The belief, if not the teaching, is that you can break any of God's commandments and laws, and Christ will get you pardoned by interceding with God on your behalf, but this isn't exactly what the Scriptures tell us.

First of all to become converted to a Christian a person must do what is written in Matthew 16:24, "Then Jesus said unto his disciples, If any man will come after me, let him deny himself, and take up his cross, and follow me. What exactly does this mean? In the first place it means give up being enslaved to the world and worldly things. That is denying himself. Then he is to take up his cross, which are the words of Christ and God, and live life the way Christ lived his life. This is further explained in verse 25, "For whosoever will save his life shall lose it: and whosoever shall lose his life for my sake shall find it. This is both a physical and spiritual verse, and needs some reasoning out. If a person just gives lip service to God and Christ, so they will not be classified as a religious freak, then spiritually they die. In the same vein, there is again to come the time when a Christian will have to confess being a Christian and will die, or deny being a Christian and live. Here again is the truth of the Holy Bible. Those who suffer the death by being cast out by friends and relatives because of the belief in Christ, and those who one day must admit to be a Christian and are slain for Christ, then both these shall find life in Christ. Christ asks the pertinent question in the next verse, "For what is a man profited if he shall gain the whole world and lose his own soul? or what shall a man give in exchange for his soul?

How many people can understand, believe, and accept that being rich with money or mammon is the worst fate that can happen to you in life. We are all taught from a early age to study, work hard, make a lot of money, and be all that you can in life. But is this good advice? The answer is no, it isn't good advice.

The formula for happiness, prosperity, and peace is in what Christ revealed to us in Matthew 6:33, "But seek ye first the kingdom of God, and his righteousness; and all these things will be added unto you. Like most things we generally have things turned around backward, saying to God, "Give me what I want first, then I'll worship you as you want me to. It just doesn't work that way, and Satan is always on hand to deceive you into thinking that because you are made rich, that God has blessed you. There has never been a rich man made by God who wasn't at first totally consumed in his worship and service to God. Solomon, David, Abraham, and Job, all were wealthy, but they were first devoted to God, then God added the blessings.

Here is the wisdom of Christ, "Lay not up for yourself treasures on earth, where moth and rust doth corrupt, and thieves break through to steal: but lay up for yourselves treasures in heaven, where neither moth nor rust doth corrupt, and where thieves do not break through to steal. For where your treasure is, there will your heart be also. Then in Matthew 6:24, "No man can serve two masters: for either he will hate the one, and love the other; or he will hold to the one, and despise the other. Ye cannot serve God and mammon. He goes on to say in Matthew 19:23 and 24, "Then said Jesus unto his disciples, Verily I say unto you, That a rich man shall hardly enter into the kingdom of heaven. And again I say unto you, it is easier for a camel to go through the eye of a needle, that for a rich man to enter into the kingdom of God.

Since this is the absolute truth, then our belief in money is a false belief put there by Satan to deceive us away from righteousness, truth, and God. Having found out the truth, that wealth just about assures us a place in hell in Hades, how many would be willing to give up their treasure? Isn't the thought there that somehow we'll get by after we leave earth? That somehow we'll be able to convince Christ and God that money didn't corrupt us, and that we did only good works, and did not fall to Satan's wiles?

Another misconception about Christ is that he was a meek, gentle person, who never was angered, and who only spoke kinds words to people, and this view point destroys the reality of Christ. In his ministry Christ was a fiery preacher taking to task all mankind, and telling them, even while he showed them mercy in their healings, of the terrible wrong doings they were committing. It could be compared to a doctor of today lecturing you about how you are destroying health, while treating your illness. Here are some prime examples of how Jesus chastised and did show a display or temper in dealing in the world. It has to be remembered that Jesus, even though he was God the Son, did not bring his powers to earth as many think, but demonstrated to man, that by asking the Father in heaven, all things would be done.

In Matthew 16:23, we read, "But he turned and said unto Peter, Get thee behind me Satan: thou art an offense unto me: for thou savorest not the things that be of God, but those that be of men. Those ar e pretty harsh words to some one you are trying to train to represent you in the world, especially the disciple you are going to rely on to be the foundation of the church, belief, and religion.

One day on the sabbath, Saturday, the disciples went through a corn field and picked corn to eat, and the Pharisees, one of the two major sects of the Jewish religion, saw them doing this, and said, Behold, thy disciples do that which is not lawful to do upon the Sabbath day.

Jesus then went on as to how David ate the shewbread which it wasn't lawful for him to do, and how priests work on the sabbath and are blameless. The in Matthew 12:11 is recorded, "And he said unto them, What man shall there be among you, that shall have one sheep, and if it fall into a pit on the sabbath day, will he not lay hold on it and lift it out? How much then is a man than a sheep? Wherefore it is lawful to do well on the sabbath days.

In the United States of America, and other Christian nations, Sunday was recognized as the sabbath, because after the crucifixion, the disciples were afraid of the Jews, and changed to meet on Sunday rather than Saturday, and this is established in John 20:19, "Then the same day at evening, being the first day of the week, when the doors were shut where the disciples were assembled for fear of the Jews, came Jesus and stood in the midst, and saith unto them, Peace be unto you. We call Saturday and Sunday the week end, but Sunday is the first day of the week, though most have in their mind it is the last day of the week. We look at Monday as being the first day, because it is the first workday of the week. Since God declared the sabbath to be the last day, which would be Saturday, this day is used by the Jews as the sabbath, and in Jesus recognizing the gathering of the disciples on Sunday, he was acknowledging the change, and allowed it to stand.

This is apparent, in the fact that when he at first appeared to them on a Sunday, the day he ascended to God, he returned eight days later, another Sunday, Jesus came again to the disciples. This assures that either Saturday or Sunday can used to worship God and Christ officially, but common sense would dictate recognizing every day as the Lord's day, and he should thereby be honored and worshipped every day, and not just one day a week. The reason for the sabbath was so man could rest from his labors, even as God rested on the seventh day of creation, which may not yet be completed.

In another episode to show his human qualities is written in Matthew 21:18 and 19, "Now in the morning as he returned into the city, he hungered. And when he saw a fig tree in the way, he came to it, and found nothing thereon, but leaves only, and said unto it, Let no fruit grow on thee henceforward for ever. and presently the tree withered away. Is this not explosive in temperament?

Then in Matthew 21 :12 is what is said to those in the temple, "And he said unto them, It is written, My house shall be called the house of prayer; but ye have made it a den of thieves. He had already overthrown the money changers tables and the seats of those who sold doves. This surely isn't a meek and mild man's actions, but one of fierce and righteous anger.

There is a final thing that can be said about Christ, and it is this. He is just as misunderstood by man today as is God, and the Holy Ghost. It is unfortunate that few will ever grow spiritually and mentally enough to know the absolute truth given us by these three deities who is so anxious for our well being, and our pursuit toward becoming the children of God. Each individual, particularly the male of each family, should fulfill the responsibility of seeing and knowing that each family member is educated and live to God and Christ's expectation, by letting the Holy Ghost lead them along the pathway of life. This can only be done by cutting the bond between worldly pursuits, and pleasure, and devoting that time to God, Christ, and the Holy Ghost. Who is there that cannot spare thirty minutes a day in the study of God's word? Who is there that cannot take the time to pray not only for deliverance, guidance, and personal pleasures, but give thanks for the blessings each receives daily from God? Is there a reason we cannot silently voice our thanks throughout the day to God? Is there any reason we cannot put down the magazine we read for enjoyment, and read a few verses from the Holy Bible? What is there that keeps a person from committing their lives to the service of God and Christ? A lot of the answers are forthcoming as we peer into the future through the Scriptures, and figure out what is ahead for the Universe, earth, and man.

CHAPTER 6

Prelude to the End

Over the centuries there has been all kinds of predictions about whether or not an end time is to come, how it will happen, and when it will happen. As with most things, it has gotten completely confused because of the way the information has become distorted. The answer is simple enough. Understanding that the law of life spans is still in effect, there is to come a time when the Universe, and earth will come to an end time, and man must live through this time in order to become children of God. That's going to be a tough order, but we are shored up by what is recorded in Isaiah 66:22, "For as the new heavens and the new earth which I shall make, shall remain before me, saith the Lord, so shall your seed, and your name remain. These should be encouraging words, but to get to this status, there must be a lot of sifting out, and refining of man, for man to be worthy of such consideration. Too many believe our troubles ended when Christ came to serve as the last blood sacrifice for the atonement of man's sins, but that saving is conditional upon our changing to abide in the law and ethics of God, and not man. So far the world has not done this, and man's atrocities against God are becoming more manifest each day.

There is today the belief that the ages of human history will continue to unfold, but that the world is without end. This defies reasoning in as much as everything on earth, and everything known to exist in the Universe has a life span, so when it is said, "World without end there is a misconception, because this world will come to the end, and God will create all things new, including earth, and man will have been refined to being as he should, a worthy child of God.

What then is to be the signs of when the earth is to end? This question has been asked by just about everyone who has lived, and Christ's disciples also asked Jesus what would be the signs of his return in the end time of earth? Jesus then went on to tell them the different things that would be taking place at the end time, when he would come back and wrest control of earth away from Satan's grasp. There are at least four major divisions of things that are going to occur, and they in some cases all occur simultaneously, and at others, one division is predominant. Religion and social beliefs, geopolitics, governments and national trends, physical events occurring against earth from within and without, and physical events occurring in the Universe.

The first thing Christ told them is recorded in Matthew 24:4, "Take heed that no man deceive you. It has already been put forth how the whole world, and each person is deceived to some extent, and this indicative of what Christ is referring to. Deception from the outside, like when Satan challenged Eve by saying, "You shall surely not die, and wherein Satan knew what God meant, but Eve didn't, and yet submitted herself to Satan's control, is one form. Self deception, such as believing you can have your cake and eat it too, or that you can be rich, and still make it to heaven, is a good example of self deceiving. There is also the master deceivers, like those in science who stubbornly cling to the theory of evolution, and the big bang, knowing they are untrue, but peddle them as the truth to the unsuspecting public of the world. And there is the deception of those in politics, saying one thing and doing another. And worse than all are the preachers, ministers, and lay persons teaching the doctrine of men and not God's. These have done more to discourage people away from God and Christ, and into the arms of the atheist or secular belief.

The only rectifying effect available to man is to read,

understand, and let the Holy Ghost teach the meaning in the Holy Bible, and this is each individual's responsibility, and not the churches', the ministers', nor other individuals' responsibility. Each must take it upon themselves to seek a closer alliance with God, and to learn as much about God and his ways, as is possible. There is no excuse from shirking this responsibility, and God will hold the person accountable for not doing this. It comes down to this. If you are deceived, it is because you have not sought the truth of God. "For many shall come in my name, saying, I am Christ; and shall deceive many. This verse is evidenced in all quarters of life, and throughout the whole world, but here is the whole truth about it. Many profess to be Christians, and many profess to be Jews, but this is only lip service given to Christ and God, and it is based upon it being fashionable to be religious. Here's what Christ said about it. "This people draweth nigh unto me with their mouth, and honoreth me with their lips: but their heart is far from me. How can a person declaring to be a Christian, have an abortion and say it is of no consequence? How can a leader of a nation commit himself to lying, and then say he is Christian? A Christian does not murder the unborn, and a Christian does not lie. These things are of the heart, and if the heart be evil, the whole body is evil, and this is an offense to God and Christ. The whole world lives in deception, and labors under the enslavement to the deception, and the only reprieve is through the truth of God and Christ, delivered to every person by the Holy Ghost. He is the Instructor and Comforter of man, but how can we learn if we do not listen to him? In Matthew 24:6, Christ shifts away from religious belief to political actions that are to occur on earth. "And ye shall hear of wars, and rumors of war: see that ye be not troubled; for all these must come to pass, but the end is not yet.

This provides us an insight into the history and the comparison of when the end time might come, however vague it may seem. Most would believe there has always been wars, and there will always be wars, and that's a fair assessment, but in the annals of man's history, the twentieth century will become recognized as the century of war. In this time period has been two world wars, and many armed conflicts. On any given day there were 15 to 20 wars going on throughout the world.

This trend is being carried over into the twenty first century, and is going to increase in the amount of armed conflicts going on at the same time. This upheaval is based upon three religious - political - cultural stratagems being employed in the world. The Judaic religion is trying to maintain a toehold in the world, even while trying to appease the Islamic which maintain the posture that Israel must die.

The secular segment of the population throughout the world are banding together in the scientific, government, education, and commerce fields to eliminate the Christian belief. This is supported by the communist movement in China, North Korea, and elsewhere in the world like Cuba, and Afghanistan. This is basically the merging of the Communist and socialist ideas of government, leading to the New World Order, a single world government, and enslavement the people to the communist - socialist life style. Out of the New World Order concept comes the opposing government now taking shape in Europe.

While this is all going on today, the Islamic religion is pushing toward its goal of being the dominant religion in the world, by using the force of terrorism where it is deemed necessary. If this seems to be a mad, mad world, you are correct in the assumption.

It isn't enough to just say wars are going on, or national interests is what is causing the upheaval, but it requires a comprehensive look at the ingredients going together, to make the world a very dangerous place to live in, and a very dangerous life to be in.

We start by looking at the situation in the mid east today, where Israel is confronted by the Palestinians in the country, and by the Arab nations which border her. Two things have to be decided. Is Israel the rightful owner of the land she occupies? Secondly, why can't this be worked out peacefully? These are the two greatest questions about this hot spot, and though there are simple answers to the questions, not one person in the world seems to be aware of the answers, or how to proceed.

Is Israel entitled to the land she now owns? The answer is yes. If it is recalled, up to Abraham the covenant God made with Abraham is that this land would be given to Abraham's seed, through Isaac, for ever. Let's review what was said to Abraham by God. It has to be remembered that before God changed Abram's name to Abraham, he had fathered a child named Ishmael from Hagar, the hand maid of Abram's wife Sarai. In this he said two things about Ishmael. He would have many offspring (the Arab nations) and that his hand would be against every man, and every man's hand against him, and that he would dwell among his brethren, which means they would be adjoining countries.

After he changed Abram's name to Abraham, and Sarai to Sarah, he made this covenant. We read it in Genesis 17:7, "And I will establish my covenant between me and thee and thy seed after thee in their generations for an everlasting covenant, to be a God unto thee. And I will give unto thee, and to thy seed after thee, the land wherein thou art a stranger, all the land of Canaan, for an everlasting possession; and I will be their God.

It is then understood, that though as Abram the Arab nations were born out of Abram, that when God changed his name to Abraham, Isaac was born to bring forth the Jew nations. The name change separates the fatherhood of Abram from the fatherhood of Abraham, and yet meets the truth where in God told Abram that he would be the father of many nations.

God told Abraham that Isaac was to have a wife from his own family, the descendants of Shem the son of Noah, and it is out of Abraham's brother Nahor, that Rebekah was born, and became the wife of Isaac.

Isaac had two sons, one was a red hairy person called Esau, and the other was a farmer called Jacob, and Jacob being the younger got Esau to swear away his birth right, and this fulfilled the prophecy of Genesis 25:23, "And the Lord said unto her, Two nations are in thy womb, and two manner of people shall be separated from thy bowels; and the one people will be stronger than the other people; and the elder shall serve the younger. What happened to bring this about was when Isaac was dying, and he sent Esau out to hunt for venison for him, and Isaac could not see well. Rebekah sent Jacob out to get two goats, and she prepared a meal. In Genesis 27:19, Jacob goes into Isaac and Isaac asks who he is. "And Jacob said unto his father, I am Esau thy first born: I have done according as thou badest me: arise, I pray thee, sit and cat of my venison that thy soul might bless me. Isaac did bless Jacob, and this made hatred in Esau rise toward Jacob, because he lost his first born rights. Isaac did give Esau this blessing in Genesis 27:40, "And by thy sword shalt thou live, and serve thy brother; and it shall come to pass when thou shalt have the dominion, that thou shalt break his yoke from off thy neck.

Isaac, told Jacob that he was not to marry outside his brethren, and Jacob went back to his mother's brother, Bethuel, and Esau went to Ishamael and took two wives that were out of Ishmael. Jacob wound up with two wives, Leah and Rachel, who were sisters. Out of Leah came Reuben, Simeon, Levi, and Judah. And out of Rachel's hand maiden Bilhah came Dan, Naphtali. Then out of Zilpah, Leah's hand maid, was born to Jacob Gad, and the Asher. Then out of Leah again came Issachar, and then Zebulun, and finally out of Rachel came Joseph. He also had one daughter called Dinah.

It then came to pass that Jacob took all that was his and left Laban and Laban pursued after him, and they wound up making a covenant by piling up stones, and it is recorded in Genesis 31:52, "This heap be a witness, and this pillar be witness, That I will not pass over this heap to thee, and that thou shalt not pass over this heap and this pillar unto me for harm.

Jacob sent for his brother Esau, planning to share with him some of the things he had acquired, but when his servants returned they told him Esau was coming with four hundred men.

In the night Jacob took his two wives, and their servants and his eleven sons, and crossed the brook Jabbok, and there he had to wrestle a man all night until daybreak. At last the man said, it's getting daybreak so let me go, and Jacob said not until you bless me. Then is Genesis 32:28, "And he said, Thy name shall be called no more Jacob, but Israel: for as a prince hast thou power with God and with men, and hast prevailed. This is how the name Israel rose to importance.

Esau now arrives with 400 men, and Jacob, now Israel, divided the children into the wives and handmaidens, and he sent them all out ahead except he and Rachel and their children were at the rear of the column. Esau surprised Jacob, by showing his love toward his brother.

We go now to Genesis 35: 11, God has changed his name to Israel, and now God speaks to Israel, "And God said unto him, I am God Almighty: be fruitful and multiply; a nation and a company of nations shall be out of thee, and kings shall come out of thy loins. And the land which I gave Abraham and Isaac, to thee I will give it, and to thy seed after thee will I give the land. Here again God is fulfilling the covenant and the promise he made to Abraham.

We now have to follow the line of Joseph, because he is of the line of descent of the Jews. The final words of Joseph is recorded in Genesis 49:24, "1 die: and God will surely visit you, and bring you out of this land unto the land he sware to Abraham, to Isaac, and to Jacob. Because of the different circumstances, where Joseph had brought all his people into Egypt, they were now enslaved to the Egyptians. We read this in Exodus 1: 11, "Therefore they did set over them taskmasters to afflict them with their burdens. And they built for Pharaoh treasure cities Pithom and Raamses.

Just about everyone is aware that Moses led the Jews out of captivity and they wandered in the wilderness. Now in Exodus 13:5, God speaks again, "And it shall be when the Lord shall bring you into the land of the Canaanites, and the Hittites, and the Amorites, and the Hivites, and the Jebusites, which he sware unto thy fathers to give thee, a land flowing with milk and honey, that thou shalt keep this service in this month. Now the ownership of the land starts to be conditional, and these are the conditions. God is to be the only God recognized in the Jews, they are to be circumcised, and they are to honor the day and month they came out of Egypt.

Then in Exodus Moses is given the rest of the covenant in Exodus 23:31,32, and 33, "And I will set thy bounds from the Red sea even unto the sea of the Philistines, and from the desert unto the river: for I will deliver the inhabitants of the land into your hand: and thou shalt drive them out before thee. Thou shalt make no covenant with them, nor with their gods. They shall not dwell in thy land, lest they make thee sin against me: for if thou serve their gods, it will surely be a snare unto thee.

The full covenant is further explained there should be no marriages between the Jews and the people occupying Canaan, and other social type restrictions. The point about all this history is this. Since God owns the planet, he is entitled to give away anything on the planet he wishes to give away, beyond what any man might believe. The United States would never dream of giving the land back to the American Indian, nor would Canada or any other Christian Caucasian nation in the world, because the bestowing of the land to these nations is based upon God's promise to Abraham of his seed being the mighty nations of the world, and he has kept that word through the Christian movement.

The nation of Israel is to be a nation unto itself, a reservoir of God's people, kept pure in genetic descent by marriage through generations to the descendants of Shem, down through Abraham, Isaac, and Joseph. This remnant of Jews are to abide in the covenant with God in order to own and occupy the land in question today. Since 1946, when the Jews returned to their homeland, there has been a constant struggle for them to retain their freedom, and their right to the land, and up to now, they have pretty well succeeded with the help of the United States, Britain, Canada, Australia, and the other Caucasian nations making up the twelve tribes of Israel.

Understanding the inborn hatred coming from the time of Ishmael, the father of the Arab nations, brings to front why there can never be a lasting peace in the mid east until Christ returns to settle it once and for all. The consternation of the nations of the world concerning the mid east is not understood because no one has looked at the history and background of the situation, and understand that this confrontation is two things. God's presence is to be felt through Israel's abiding in the terms of the covenant, and Satan's presence is to be felt through the Palestinians and the efforts of Iraq. The serious problem in the mid east that is overlooked by the United States and other nations, which are trying to arrange a mid east accord, is they are not using the model God has given for the ownership of Israel, and how it is God's right to enforce that his will be done. This leads to what is happening in nearby Iraq.

Iraq was Babylon of old, and by Biblical prophecy is to become a force to be reckoned with in the end time, and we are seeing the emergence of that power right today before our eyes, and yet, not a single politician recognizes the coming danger.

155

Iraq is slowly gaining power and prestige through help of her Arab neighbors and China, and despite the constant over flying and strikes against the radar and anti aircraft batteries, she is keeping the United Nations inspection teams out of her land, and is rebuilding her factories to make nuclear, biological, and chemical weapons, which will be used in the last war on earth.

The dam of sanctions against Iraq has been breached, and it has to be understood, that despite the hardship in the land, these people will not turn away from their goal to make a bid at re-establishing the Babylonian empire, and destroy all the nations of the Jews, which means all Jewish and Christian (Caucasian) nations. This comes from the same jealous hatred that started from Ishamael toward Isaac, and has been carried forward, generation to generation, and will not have an end to it until Christ comes to reclaim the planet.

Iraq is to form a coalition of Arab nations that will one day rival the seated government of the world, and that government is rising in Europe today.

It has been shown why the Jews are entitled to the land they inhabit. and why the Palestinians should be ousted from the land. This is what God says to do under the covenant he made with Abraham, Isaac, Joseph and Moses, but in ignorance do nations like the United States interfere with God's judgment, setting their own agenda before God's will and determination. This political pressure applied to Israel to give part of the land to the Palestinians is not of God, but of Satan, and is to have dire consequences for Israel, and the nations making up the twelve tribes of Israel, notably the Christian Caucasian nations in the world.

Part of the misunderstanding by the leaders of the nations is through their ignorance of what the Holy Scriptures say is to happen in the world. The prophecy of the wars, and rumors of wars is becoming more pronounced each day as hot spots on earth arise. The prophecy of Matthew 24:7 is well underway, and this is evidenced by what has happened recently in the world. Nation against nation is explained as in WWII, but kingdom against kingdom refers to the struggle of nations today and in the recent past that have or had civil wars. The USSR failed, and provided a contingent of nations going to war for their own independence, and everyone believed this would be the end of Russia as a world power, but this isn't true, because of what the Holy Bible says will happen.

Nations like Korea, which have become two nations in a nation, Viet Nam in which the atheist government won over the superior forces of the United States, and the most recent the civil wars raging in Africa that came about by the replacement of the minority Caucasian government by majority Black government. Although unrecognized by the diplomats, and politicians of the world, what is happening today in Africa is going to have a great world impact in the not too distant future.

In this time period is the loss of the Suez canal by the British, the abandonment of Gibraltar, and the great cities under English control on the main land of China, the United States surrender of the Panama canal, now under the control of a communist company out of China, and the withdrawing of American troops from strategic locations such as Okinawa, the Philippine islands, and other critical locations that cost thousands of American lives to recapture and hold in WWII.

Communist China is barely off the ground as a rising super power, but she has already declared that in the next year or so, she will claim all land within two thousand miles of her shores, and this is to mean that Taiwan and the Philippine islands will come under her control. With her control of the strategic water ways, entrances, and ports, and in particular the Panama canal, she will be able to stop or deter and delay the vital shipment of goods from and to the United States. The flow of goods from far east to places on the east coast will have to be routed around the tip of South America, and those goods from Europe going to places like San Francisco will have to be routed around the tip of South America, when China decides to start choking America's strength.

China's influence is now being extended to Iraq, where she is providing the necessary underground communication cables (fiber optics) which will stifle American and British retaliatory strikes against the radar and communication centers which they do today with impunity.

It can then be understood, that the nation against nation, kingdom against kingdom has over spread the world today, and as Christ told his disciples these are only some of many signs of his return. It does require understanding and sorting out the trend, and not just isolated incidents. It is only when dealing with the question in Israel where specific incidents will tell that the end time is very near.

In this world of plenty, there is still famine sweeping nation through nation, and at present this is only the tip of the iceberg, so to say. The climate of earth is heating up, and the desert land of the world is increasing. At the same time, the soil of earth is slowly being depleted of its ability to produce life, and even with the addition of chemicals, which further destroys earth's ability to bring forth life, the planet is starting to wax old, as the Scriptures tell us will happen. This means that in the future, probably not too distant, the earth's food supply is going to be sharply curtailed by weather, the earth's age, climate, and use of even harsher chemicals in farming. As it is now, there is a great clamor made about the starving people in Africa, but at the same time American farmers are plowing under crops because they can not get a price to repay the cost of producing the crops.

For the first time in history, America is now becoming dependent on foreign food supplies, and as the nation becomes more dependent upon these outside suppliers, America's own farming industry will slowly become nonexistent. This death has already been observed in the manufacturing of iron and steel, apparel, shoes, electronics, and more slowly is the demise of American made autos, aircraft, trains, and other forms of transportation, especially commercial ship building. The loss of agriculture will bring to the end the age of American power, and greatness, and we will be a nation dependent upon the other nations of the world.

This is already in evidence by how the Arab oil source can strangle the United States in only a few months, but is there an alternative being worked out? the answer is no, and when Iraq gets into full accord with the coalition of Arab nations, which is shortly to come about, America, and other white Christian nations are going to feel the severe crunch of power exerted against them.

Part of the famine to be endured is going to come by what is happening in the world as far as finances go. The United States has had nine years of growth without inflation, but that is ending in 2001, and the nation is beginning to slide toward the abyss of financial depression. The situation is this. Consumer spending has gone on too long without being checked, and individual debt through credit is out of sight. As the recession deepens, people are going to start losing their homes, cars, and businesses through foreclosures by the financial institutions, which are most now supported by foreign money. This financial power is going to be realized more sharply in the days to come, as will be seen in later text.

Can there be any debate about the pestilence sweeping over the world today? The new forms of influenza, mad cow disease, the scare of genetically altered food, the new forms of cancer, the spread of diseases such as Ebola, the Hanta virus, all testify that we are on the brink of the time when the world is going to suffer terribly from diseases both of man's doing, and from God through Satan. The people of Africa and India suffer greatly from pestilence, but this is going to be, and is, currently becoming extended to where every nation in the world is going to endure these diseases. Diseases once believed confined to specific areas of the world are now being felt in out of the way places. The mosquito carrying the disease like malaria in the New England states is only one example.

As more food, clothing, and other items come in from abroad under the trade agreements, more and more diseases and insects are going to be introduced into countries that never had them before. The killer bees from Africa that were taken to Brazil for study and escaped hves now invaded the southern states of this country and are becoming a danger to Americans. What should be of more concern is the apathy of the individual citizen, that shrugs off these signs with apparent indifference.

Although earthquakes are showing up in places where earthquakes were known before, there is a greater threat coming, and is stems from the extraction of the oil and minerals from deep underground and undersea locations. Two things will result from this, and they are beginning to take shape in these days we are living in now.

The extraction of these materials from deep under the ground and under the sea, create great voids or caverns from where the material was removed, and though this isn't apparent right at the moment, in one violent moment, because of the planet trying to compress tighter under gravity, these large voids and caverns are going to collapse, shaking the entire earth in one gigantic and devastating quake. It can be seen that while this doesn't seem to be a problem at the moment, it's time to hang on your hat for the ride of all times, as earth makes ready to go into its first death throes. Christ sums it up as, "All these are the beginning of sorrows.

In Matthew 24:9 is recorded, "Then they shall deliver you up to be afflicted, and shall kill you: and you shall be hated of all nations for my names sake. This is a dual prophecy, and we know that the disciples of Christ were killed because they brought the word of God, the absolute truth, into the darkness of earth, and people simply didn't like the light of truth. It is no different today, and while the text is confined to the United States, it applies as well to the Christian nations which make up the realm of the twelve tribes of Israel.

The reason the United States, Britain, and her possessions rose and maintained world power structure as great powers was because of the strict compliance of being nations serving as the disciples of Christ, and in obedience of God's commandments, ethics, and doctrine. What is being witnessed today is the decline in that world greatness, and a loss of power, majesty, and glory. The reason this is happening is from the same cause of that which is happening in Israel today, the abandonment of God's word, for the wisdom of man. No where on earth is the struggle prophesied in Matthew 24:10 greater than in the United States of America today.

The social, economic, religious, educational, and government influences in the United States of America has been diverted away from God and Christ, toward the New World Order, secularism, and false beliefs, and this is to continue on for some time to come.

The United States and Britain are the offspring of Joseph, part of the twelve tribes of Israel, and they have received the fulfillment of the prophecy written in Genesis 17:4, "As for me, behold, my covenant is with thee, and thou shalt be a father of many nations. Then in verse 6, he says, "And I will make thee exceedingly fruitful, and I will make nations of thee, and kings shall come out of thee. When the domain of England was disassembled, by the United States becoming and independent nation, followed by Canada, Australia, and the other free nations of English descent, God had fulfilled the prophecy and his part of the covenant. It is that the people and government of these lands do not recognize their heritage and their genetic link to Abraham, and therefore are not aware of either God's covenant with them, or what these nations need to do retain that covenant with God.

The trend going on in the supposedly civilized nations of the world, America and England, can be defined as a turn away from God and Christ, toward the secular and atheist belief, and the action of trying to establish that man does not need a God above them, and that man himself is able to administer the affairs of the planet. This short sighted view is the result of the teaching of evolution, and the big bang theory, and the discarding the straight moral ethics of God and Christ, and the putting into its place the morality of Satan.

This trend is the most dangerous trend on earth today because it leads to enslavement of the entire world, and in that enslavement there will be only the gnashing of teeth, and the wailing of misery from the people. If you think the Jews have suffered greatly from the time they were in bondage to Egypt, to the concentration camps, and the holocaust suffered in WWII these woes will be mild when compared to what the world is going to undergo under the yoke of slavery that will come through the coming world government now rising in Europe.

Part of the whole scenario is the falling away of the Christian belief, and the belief in God, and we are seeing this happen right here in the United States today, where prayer has been banned from schools, religious scenes barred from public property, the banning of religious meetings or worship on public lands. Include in this such horrendous crimes against God as the right to murder the unborn through abortion, the acceptance of homosexual behavior, the sudden decision of letting women run the nation's government, schools, churches, and industry, and soon to be, the armed forces of the United States. It can be said with good authority, that the United States is starting its slide toward oblivion.

This segment ends with what Christ says in Matthew 24:13, "But he that shall endure unto the end, the same shall be saved. This is Christ's last plea to all people to wake up, stand up, and be counted on his side, for the world is going to shortly pass away, but Christ and his loyal followers are not going to perish. Each person has to look at their own past record, and decide quickly whether they are going to buckle down and do the things God and Christ has told them to do, or whether they will dawdle along and let the end time engulf them, and thereby lose out on the chance to be saved. It is all up to the individual.

Matthew 24:22 is quite appropriate for a person to understand as we near the end time. "And except those days be shortened, there should no flesh be saved: but for the elect's sake those days shall be shortened. As it was in the day of Noah, there were the many, all except Noah and his family, who thought it was Noah who was all wet in his building of the ark, and they drowned in their own ignorance. So shall it be in the end time, and though the warning has been issued, very few will believe until it is too late. The saving ark is Jesus Christ, and those who do not get aboard now, today, will find themselves swimming and floundering in flood of the wrath of God which God is going to pour upon the whole earth very shortly.

CHAPTER 7

The Finale

The end time has been predicted by many people over the centuries, and of which none of the predictions came true, and because of this, most have shrugged off the idea that an end time will come, even though it is prophesied in the Holy Bible.

We stand at the threshold of that time, and in a matter of a short time, earth is going to enter the end time. The obvious question is, How are we to know? This requires a lot of assimilation of facts that have been pointed out so far in this book, and of what else is written in the Holy Bible about this time. Four or more scientific facts have come to light in very recent times. The first is that science has observed two galaxies passing through each other headed in opposite directions. If the Universe is expanding as indicated by scientific theory, and Biblical truth, then how is this to be explained, except that one galaxy has reached the extreme of the Universe and is rebounding back toward the center? In all models of the Universe it is an outward movement, and for a galaxy to be going in the opposite direction implies the collapse of the Universe is inevitable.

The second is that the sun is heating up, and this may indicate that it is getting toward the time when it must switch over to burning the inner gasses. It is known the sun bums about 5,000,000 tons of fuel per second, and even though its massive size (109 times that of earth) would allow a long time burn, scientists are now doubtful as to the accuracy of their theories, and their concern is over the apparent heating up of the sun, which means more fuel being used. It isn't known but it will become apparent, that if indeed the galaxy mentioned above has rebounded from the extremes of the Universe, then centrifugal force is weakening in the Universe, and gravity is increasing slightly. This might account for the sun becoming hotter under higher compression, and it accounts also that the earth is also heating up further under compression, and therefore tectonic plate movement is greater, and earthquakes more common.

The third is that in the laboratory light has been slowed down, accelerated, and actually stopped, disproving science's once held law that light was the ultimate speed, and a limitation. This destroys the time element that science used in time distance equations, and this means science is at a loss for any accuracy in the age of anything in the Universe or on earth.

The next is the concession of science that life on earth is a very unique event, and they are now starting to believe that the other planets in the Universe are just bodies in a natural descending order. There has also been the fear raised that earth is due to collide with an asteroid, or comet, or other space object in the not to distant future, and science is genuinely scared that this event can happen almost at any time. They have started a tracking program, listing all the orbits of objects that may imperil earth, and are trying to develop ideas of how to keep such a catastrophe from occurring. They center their ideas on a way to either divert the object from its collision with earth, or a way to destroy the object before it strikes earth.

These scientific concerns will become reality as we enter the end time, and there will be no doubt as you read about the end time how these things will affect each individual.

The general trend of the nations is to return to the time of the tower of Babel, and this is going to take shape in several forms, political reform, disbanding of religion, full secular education, and a financially based government.

We start with what is written In Revelation 3:7 through 11, and even though it was written to the angel of the church in

Asia, considering how the United States of America was born, and where, can give rise that since North America wasn't yet established as a nation, and the name Philadelphia was the name of a church located in Asia, it is possible that Christ is speaking to the Philadelphia wherein the promise of Abraham is to be fulfilled, and that is in Philadelphia U. S. A. Read carefully what is written, "And to the angel of the church in Philadelphia write; These things saith he that is holy, he that is true, he that hath the key of David, he that openeth and no man shutteth, and shutteth, and no man openeth. Take into consideration that few Asian states embrace the Christian religion, and add to it that the Key of David is passed among the Jews, and not to outsiders, which is another way of Christ saying the twelve tribes of Israel are the chosen people. The twelve tribes of Israel are the holy people, devoted to God and Christ, and are manifested in the Christian and Jewish faith.

The word Philadelphia means "brotherly love and this kinship is more apparent between Christian nations and Israel than is any bond between other nations. In addition to that, consider the constitution and other important legislative acts by the founding fathers of America did these in Philadelphia and under the prayer to God asking guidance from God. This is the first nation to adopt that they are a nation under God and use the motto on their money, saying "In God We Trust. When the United States of America was founded upon the Godly principles and belief, God had fulfilled the covenant he made to Abraham, Isaac, and Joseph. The Caucasian Christian nations are the nations God told Abraham he would father, and the small nation of Israel is the remnant of the seed that has not converted to honoring God's son as the Savior. Despite this, knowing the Jews to be a "stiff necked people, he is keeping the original covenant with this small state, but has switched his main emphasis from those living in Israel to the Christian nations having Christ as their leader. This explains why

America, Britain, Canada, Australia, and the other Christian nations under this umbrella has risen to the highest power, glory and wealth, and is hated by all other nations.

It continues in verse 8, "I know thy works: behold I have set before thee an open door, and no man can shut it: for thou hast a little strength, and hast kept my word, and hast not denied my name. This expression of power wealth and glory came to the family of Christian nations because of the very things said in the verse, the belief in Christ, and the telling of that to all the peoples on earth. The United States has aided more nations in the world than all other nations combined, and the generosity of the nation is known world wide. Why do you suppose everyone in the world desires to live in America? It isn't because of the climate, it isn't because of the government, and it isn't because of its wealth. The reason they want to live in America is to enjoy the peace, the tranquillity, and the ease of life America offers. The worst day and suffering of the poor in America is much milder torment than the torment of the rich in war torn nations in Africa.

In verse 9 is written, "Behold, I will make them of the synagogue of Satan, which say they are Jews and are not, but do lie; behold, I will make them to come and worship before thy feet, and to know that I have loved thee. Can there be any doubt that these nations under God and Christ are the envy of all the nations in the world, and they marvel at the strength, endurance, and prosperity, which they cannot enjoy because of their alliance with Satan. There are also the nations which try to put on the facade of having Christian and Godly ways, (which say they are Jews and are not, but do lie) and still cater to the ways of Satan rather than Christ or God. Germany is such a nation, and followed closely by France, and Italy. You can not be a Christian nation or a Godly state, and have the ambitions to be the master race, and to rule the world, and do this through atrocities. Germany has launched the new approach to forming the fourth Reich or power, and the Vatican sees this as an opportunity to establish Catholicism as the world's religion.

Revelation 3: 10, "Because thou hast kept the word of my patience, I also will keep thee from the hour of temptation, which shall come upon all the world, to try them that dwell upon the earth. Right now the United States and Britain are struggling with internal forces that is trying to push the nation into oblivion and under the rule of Satan.

The emergence of ultra liberalism, and the socialist agenda offers the biggest threats to undermine the Christian and Godly foundation of these great nations. The New World Order is the establishment of a single world government based on a single currency, and dedicated to world enslavement to Satan. Here are the different elements of evidence that support this conclusion.

The world, through the United Nations, continue to say that the only way to world peace and prosperity is by having a single world government, and that government is being set up today in Europe under the leadership of Germany. In the natural flow of things, it started becoming a reality when the American's took the American dollar off the gold standard, and let it float. This is the time when it was changed from a gold or silver certificate to a Federal Reserve note, which is incidentally an IOU. Under the gold deposit standard, there had to be so much gold on hand in Fort Knox before more money could be printed, and this made the saying throughout the world to show excellence, "It's as good as the American dollar.

This is why America is deeply in debt, some several trillion dollars or more, and we are still spending way beyond the ability of the nation to pay its debts, but that is starting to catch up with the country in 2001. The supposed life of unimagined growth and prosperity has been due to spending like we are on a drunken spree, and now the law has caught up and we're going to have to pay dearly for our actions.

STEPHEN W. ERVIN

The average American today is in hock right up to his neck, and creditors are just waiting for the balloon to burst, and they'll reap a rich profit by repossessing everything mortgaged, and reselling it at a higher price when the country begins to recover. The whole scheme is this. The house you buy, the car you buy, the motor home, the boat, the snow mobile, and other tangible goods will eventually be repossessed. The money you plunked down for it at the fit in the form of a down payment, the payments you made over the years, and the interest you paid during the life of the time you had the property, will be lost, and this means most people are going to end up paying rent, when they thought they were buying. Technically, it can be said that you own the property, but this remains only partly true, more like a conditional sales contract, that says as long as you pay you own, you stop paying we own.

The going off the gold standard, the opening up of easy credit and high private debt is only the beginning of the nightmare. The financial institutions with the cooperation of the government has started the first step toward installation of the credit / debit system, and the use of the plastic card in place of money, and the use is getting widespread. Why do you think financial organizations are willing to give a line of credit to anyone over 18 years of age, and are pushing parents to give their children their own personal credit cards? You've heard the advertising, "Got bad credit? No credit? call us for a card.

The ins and outs of it is this. They publicize that direct deposit of money owed you from the government, for pensions, retirement, or social security or disability is safer in direct deposit, more convenient, and now mandatory. By doing this, there is a paper trail of where the money came from, and where the money went to, and the government and financial institutions can use this information for their purposes. There has always been an area that the government has tried to tax, and hasn't been able to do so as of yet, but with cash slowly going out of the picture, and the plastic card replacing it for the credit debit system, a lot of the trading or bartering between private individuals will come under the scrutiny of the government, because a paper trail will be generated. At present, If a couple of kids are given a few bucks to shovel the snow off the walks, or weed the garden, there is no reported transaction, but when money eventually becomes outmoded, and the plastic in, a paper trail will be established, and the government and other interested persons can gain access. Suppose you pay less than minimum wage, or suppose you expose a person to a hazard without workman's compensation insurance, look at the accessibility to governmental offices and laws if these transactions are on paper, and otherwise goes by without notice when cash is paid. It hasn't been too long back that a law was instituted where if you had someone in to help around the house or yard, and you paid a certain amount of money, you also had to withhold tax, and pay the employers portion of Social Security tax, and you had to get a Federal tax identification number. By paying cash under the table, as the saying goes, the procedure continues, but the person cannot write off the expense, and the employee doesn't report the income. This will change as the credit /debit system gets fully installed, and cash is removed from the picture.

It might be noted, United States dollar has reigned supreme over all other currencies, but with the introduction of the new Euro dollar, the United States, the Canadian, and the Australian dollar is on the way out as world trading dollar, and the Euro will become the world dollar. Right now the Euro dollar is worth about 88 cents of American money, but it will rapidly build, as the new European Union gets better set up, and the wealth of the combined nations under the Euro dollar begins to assert its dominance.

You would think the American government would be alarmed, but they have been briefed this is only a transient stage in which money will no longer be used as a means of trade. Right now it is the foreign money keeping the United States afloat in the sea of debt it owes, but as this capital gets withdrawn, as European manufacturing, services, and commodities take over dominance in world trade, the United States is going to drown in the sea of debt they are building today.

The multinational corporations are gobbling up other multinational corporations, such as the merger of Daimler, Chrysler, and Nissan motors. In the next few years it will be the German car that will be the top billed car throughout the world. Other such takeovers, such as in the communications, banks, and energy companies show the trend is toward one gigantic corporation emerging in each category, and finally one corporation will own everything in the world.

As time-tested American companies fail, new multinational companies fill the vacancy making America more reliant of foreign goods and money. This places American financial institutions in a precarious position unless they merge with more stable overseas economies. Behind this is the World Bank carefully manipulating world events, trade flow, and worldwide wealth distribution. Want a war? Consult the World Bank. Want food for your nation? Consult the World Bank. Need Arms for protection? Consult the World Bank. The financial health of Christian nations is waning in favor of the European Union, but that is only the first thread of a rope of events designed to sell these nations into slavery. There's a lot more.

Not too long ago Canada decided to disarm the private citizen of the nation, and the private citizen say now it was the worst thing they could have done in today's world, and they regret having turned in their firearms. Britain has long banned firearms from the citizens, and the United States effort to disarm the private citizen is well underway, with new legislation almost every year providing for more gun control, and easier confiscation of private firearms. There has been a lot argued on both sides about guns, the harm they do, and why they should be banned in the United States, but no one champions the truth about why firearms are essential in the free world, especially America.

The American constitution allows for an armed militia, and this is above and beyond the armed forces of the United States of America. The militia talked about in the constitution is the silent majority of Americans who own guns, and have them only as a deterrent against crime being committed against them, and for the prevention of a foreign power to occupy the United States.

Part of any planned invasion of a country is to disarm the private citizen so occupation is made easier for the troops to occupy the land. Like the financial picture, removal or destruction of local currency is one of the first ways to internally destroy a nation, and then disarming the nation prepares the nation for occupation by foreign troops. The founders of the nation knew this very well, and provided the contingency of America having a silent militia, armed private citizens who would come to America's defense even if the armed forces of the nation were to be defeated. An armed hostile nation cannot be successfully occupied, because of the under lying task of having a guard for each person, and to have that guard constantly at risk, defies reason. The second reason the silent militia is in place is to safeguard America from becoming a dictatorial state. Even if a plot developed where the armed forces decided to join a dictatorial leader in a bid to take the country, the silent militia, the average citizen owning a gun acts as a deterrent against such aggression.

There are many news accounts about the militias forming today, and the truth is they are forming because the trend of the government is toward surrender to the New World Order, and these groups are forming in objection to that trend. There are several hundred of them now formed, and their membership is growing in number. In some, leadership has fallen into the hands of radicals looking for their own agenda, and not the safety of the nation, but these are few. What triggered the sudden explosion of militias to form?

No more than four or five years ago it was in the plan to take the land from US highway 2 in Washington state, reaching from Winthrop, Washington to the coast, and northward into British Columbia, and cede it to the United Nations as a United Nations park, removing the ownership, and control of this land from the two nations, and giving the United Nations sovereign control. This meant that foreign troops could be stationed on this land. It's not hard to see how this posed a dire threat to the United States, and Canada, and the people in the northwest protested loudly enough the government put off taking such action. Instead they used the southwest desert and the south as a place to hold war games, where foreign troops would be deployed in mock invasions for training. The conspiracy in this is to get the American people used to seeing foreign troops, and thereby not pay attention, when the time comes for foreign occupation. Along with this is the new concept that American troops will now serve under foreign officers, and this was demonstrated where a German officer was the commanding officer at a base in Texas.

The influx of foreign troops, the violation of law having American troops serve under foreign officers, and the apparent give away of part of American land to foreign powers, caused the silent militia to start banding together in a loose confederation, in opposition the near treasonable actions going on in the government. The retreat away from rapidly implementing the New World Order movement in the United States has been slowed by the rise of the opposing silent militia, but it is far from dead. Though the implementation has slowed, we are still moving slowly toward being taken into the single world government through the legislative actions of those sworn to keep America strong, free, and separate from other nations.

The recent influx of foreign money into the politics of this nation isn't exactly new, but is getting better coverage by the media, and the discovery that our moral ethics individually has decayed, and it's being found out that most politicians can be bought by foreign money. The system is in and it is clearly visible when you ask the question of why would a person spend many millions of dollars for a job that pays only $200,000 annually as salary? Who in their right mind would leave being the CEO of a major corporation to serve at less than half pay in government? Can it not be agreed there must be some hidden incentive to go to such lengths?

For the private citizens entering into the field of politics full of the ideals that they can do some good in Washington for the people of the nation, their hopes are soon squashed by the manipulators of the system, and they are induced to join the system, and not make waves. For those honest enough to refuse the bribery, they are forced to either resign, or are publicly shamed and damaged to the extent their career in government service is ended.

There isn't anyone alive that doesn't have one or more dishonorable things in their past, and these are used to black mail a person into submission or out. There is no end to how deeply foreign powers have embedded themselves in American politics, from the local level to the white house.

There is a continuous railing against gun ownership, formation of an active militia, and why America needs to step down from being the super power in the world, and content ourselves to being subjective to other powers. This is demonstrated by how the United States and Britain were sucked into Kosovo by Germany, to achieve what Germany wanted, without German exposure.

Germany is the rising power in Europe, and the Christian Serbs blocked Germany's influence in that sector of the world, so the easiest way was to get rid of the current Christian leadership, and replace it with a more liberal leader who would bow to Germany's bidding. Using the pretext of their being many killing fields, where supposedly the Christian Serbs mass murdered the Albanian Moslems, the United States launched attacks against the Serbs. This is pretty unprecedented to have a Christian nation attack another Christian nation in defense of a people having the Islamic religion that says Christians must die.

After the ouster of the Christians from their homeland, in the so called killing fields, were found the bodies of Serbs slain by the Albanians, instead of being the other way round. The Serb people, have relented to the pressure of the United States and Germany, and have installed a leader now willing to capitulate to German influence and eventual control. It is evident from the news, that Germany's goal has been achieved through use of the United States.

The Albanians in Kosovo are from Albania, and this is like having Mexico insist that because a number of their people live illegally in the United States, Canada must move in to protect them from the United States ousting them. Doesn't really make much sense does it?

The armed conflict at Ruby Ridge, the Davidian complex, are two clashes between the law enforcement agencies, and the militias forming in the United States today, and the retaliation was the Oklahoma City bombing. The ultra right wing and the misguided ultra racist factions in the militia are isolated cases, but there is this to say about these factions. The more the nation goes toward liberalism, and socialism, the more member strength these type organizations will gain, and the reason is this. Socially, America was founded on the Caucasian Christians who wanted self rule, and were known as rebels by

England, even though there was a strong element of the people who wanted to stay under the rule of England. When the constitution was written, it was written under the specification that the average American was Caucasian and Christian. Blacks, Indians, and other races were not considered as Americans or Christians, and were therefore left out of the overall treatise of the founding documents. It has to be remembered the Blacks were from Africa, and had their own religion, as did the American Indians who were being dispossessed of their holdings. The thinking of that time was the Indians were savages, as were the Negroes.

The influx of people of minority races, and not of Christian belief has altered the overall makeup of America, and in a short while, if it hasn't already occurred, the combined minority population will exceed that of the Caucasian Christian population, and the United States government will be classified as an apartheid government, and will be forced to resign the control of the government by Caucasians, to the combined minorities. This is the fear that drives the narrow viewed men in the extremist militias. It can be understood why they have become extreme in their fervor against such a takeover, but this fervor cannot and should not be expressed through violence against the government or the people.

There is a misconception propagated by socialists that all people are created equal in the eyes of the Lord and in the eyes of the law, but this isn't the case at all. No two people are exactly the same, and the evidence is in the case of identical twins. They may be identical in every way except life experiences, and that is enough to make them individuals. There are no two stars in the heaven that are exactly alike, and no two cars coming off the assembly line are exactly the same. Similar is true, but exactly same, absolutely not. This is why it cannot be said that all people are equal, because equal means to the nth degree, and that is only possible in hypothetical situations or models. Each individual is of God, and is to do whatever God puts before him to do on earth, and this makes for inequality in the eyes of God.

Neither can there be equality under the law, because in making of a law, in the interpretation of the law, and in the administering of the law there are too many variables to give equality. The concept of people being equal in the eyes of God, and under the law is then not accurate enough to be the absolute truth, and has to be classified as perceived truth.

The socialist doctrine and goal is similar to the belief of the communist, in that individual rights must be surrendered for the overall good of the society. In this model, people are to be surrendered to be like the socialized insects, the bees, termites and ants, where individuals are sacrificed for the good of the colony. This is the model the world is headed toward under the New World Order.

It can be seen that two major inroads toward the destruction of a free nation has been partially met. They are destruction of the economy of the nation, and the removal of firearms from the general public. The social aspects, of implied equality of all people is a misguided and misunderstood theory to incite people to move toward the socialist rule.

There is the idea the wealth of the nation should be redistributed from the wealthy to the poor, but like so many of man's ideals they are based on a false premise. There is the old saying, and it is true, "God must love poor people because he made so many of them. Nothing could be truer said. Nowhere in the Holy Bible is man encouraged to gather material wealth, and there are many, many verses, that tell you that to serve money means to deny God, and there is no way to serve both. There is a difference between wealth and prosperity, and it is this.

Prosperity given of God is the fulfillment of basic needs to sustain life, and to complete the work God has scheduled the person to do on earth. Wealth is the disregard of God's work on earth by the individual while they lust for worldly possessions. Two entirely different formats, and to do one means to disregard the other.

The third event occurring driving this nation, and other Christian nations into the hands of foreign powers pushing the New World Order is the narrow interpretation of the enacted laws, and the constitution, when dealing with cases in the Supreme Court of the United States. In their written opinions, the Justices have failed miserably to carry out justice, and has ascribed to legality under the law. It is thereby consented that murder of the unborn by abortion is legal, and not punishable under the law. The intent of banning prayer or gathering on public land for the purpose of religious celebration or worship, may seem civil and right to some, but is that not agreeing with atheists who brought the lawsuit? Is praying to God and Christ a breach of American law if we are a nation under God?

Suppose for a moment a person closes his eyes before the classroom and silently prays for God's guidance in teaching the class, has that person broken the law? Even if the prayer is uttered aloud, is that not within the constitutional freedom of speech? No one is for forced prayer, and no one is for designated prayer to a specific deity, but neither is anyone to be restricted from speaking to their God at any time. The communication between man and God is a freedom granted by God, and cannot be usurped by man's laws. It should therefore be understood that those wishing to participate in a prayer to their God may do so, and those wishing to abstain from prayer may also do so. There is no requirement under the constitution to either, demand prayer, nor forbid prayer.

Critics claim there should be a separation between church and state, and this is also a very misunderstood proposition of the constitution. The founders of this country were well aware that most people in the forming nation were Christian, but of different denominations. It was therefore concluded that no specific denomination could be set by congress as the national church. They were also very aware that those drawing up the paperwork of the nation, established the nation on Christian principles, ethics, and doctrine, because they were Christian. Isn't it true that if a Christian is elected to congress his viewpoint is going to be that of a Christian, and if a Jew is elected to congress isn't his viewpoint going to be that of a Jew? It is just as true that an atheist is elected to congress he puts forth the atheist view, or if a person is of Islamic religion they would put forth the Islamic view. How then can the state be free of religion? To advance the atheist belief is just as wrong as to advance a religious belief, so there is virtually no way to separate church from state, nor was it ever God's intention that we should do so. The promoters of atheism, which are the ultra liberal socialists, have attacked on every front in America law to force the nation to secular or atheist belief. Science, being atheist, promotes its atheism through the theories and slanted material fed to the educational facilities of the nation, to the government, and to commerce. It can be said with good assurance, that science, government, education, and commerce are all under the control of atheists.

There is a steady outcry of foul whenever the religious right attacks the liberal socialist left in the nation, and the media howls in delight whenever a conservative slips and falls in the public arena. Just as quick are they ready to jump to the defense of any liberal cause or person. It is no longer fashionable to be a good staunch loyal Christian American.

This is shown in the classic illustrations of how the different people in the nation refer to themselves. There is the American Indian, there is the American Jew, and there is also the African American, the Mexican American, the Asian American. In the former the devotion denotes America as the adopted nation first, followed by the cultural nation. In the last it is devotion to the cultural nation first, and citizenship in America as last. Of the races seeking integration into the Caucasian race, there is only this to say. God separated the people by race and by language that they not intermix and return to the time of the tower of Babel. God has very strenuously dictated to the twelve tribes of Israel they were not to marry outside their race and people. Is this bigotry? No. It is doing what God has commanded the twelve tribes of Israel to do if they are to preserve their heritage God swore to Abraham, Isaac, and Joseph. How can that be called bigotry or racism? The socialist idea that one shoe fits all just won't work. The American Indian is entitled to his gods, and the right to serve and worship them in their custom. The Blacks are entitled to pursue whatever religious belief, and use what ever customs they desire. The Jew, including the Christians are entitled also to do as their God commands them, and when God says they are not to take unto them wives of other beliefs or people, nor are they to marry into other cultures and beliefs, they are only following the commandments of their God. This extends to the trouble in Israel today allowing the Palestinians to live in their land, against the covenant which God made with them, saying , these people will not inhabit your land. Israel will pay for letting the Palestinians live in the land given to Israel by God, but in the long run then, who is the loser but Israel for not obeying God's commandments?

There can be no argument about marriages between the Black race and the Asian races, because their extraction is different from the Caucasian Jew extraction. No specific Bible verses prohibits marriage between these two races, but of either the Mongolian race, or the Negroid race, marriage into the Caucasian Jewish race is forbidden under the edicts that God laid on the people as they prepared to enter the promised land after their forty years in the wilderness. There need not be, nor will there ever be a single race of people on earth, for as God has preserved the genetic line from Adam and Eve down through Jacob, so will he continue to preserve his chosen people and chosen line. No man can or dare argue with God about this.

Most are unwilling to understand that in the oneness, in the singularity of there being only one race, one government one religion, one measurement, or one of anything, there is only enslavement, and the promoters of the socialist movement use various forms of deceit to trap the unwary. A island stranded man, given the company of another man, regardless of race, creed, or color will accept and cohabit the island in peaceful intent. They need not live together to share, nor do they have to be at each others beckon and call, but they habituate in peaceful co-existence and without malice. This relationship does not change until another party is introduced onto the island.

The same is true with cultures. Cultures can be endured by different people in a land, but it is when there is a forceful intent to either invade into the other culture, or change the other culture, disharmony erupts. This is what happened to the American Indian when the whites went through the land, changing everything to suit them, instead of letting the Indians stay within their own culture and way of life.

The ongoing struggle between the Black people of this nation, and of the other cultures of this nation is of the same complexity. If any culture is to live alongside another culture, there must be an understanding of a silent non aggression pact, but also there can be no intrusion from one culture into another.

It is the forces of evil, the forces wanting control of the world, that create the conflicts and bitterness between the races and cultures. What has to be understood is what is said about it by God, and how he separated the people to preserve the three major races, and the establishment of the minor races. It has never been his intent to have a single race of people, and this is evident by his giving to the different races and cultures, lands for each, and the freedom propagate their own nations and cultures.

The Negroid race is blessed with the land of Africa, the Mongoloid with Asia, and the Caucasian the other lands and nations they now have under their control. There is no such thing as our land is better than yours, or your land is better than ours, but only jealousy invented because of greed.

By causing strife in the different races it is a matter of dividing and conquering, and we see this occurring in Africa today, where the Islamic is converting those nations to Islamic belief under terrorism and any other method they choose. The wedge in American society, the alienation of the Black population, is come about by the militant forces within the culture which believe they are entitled to get something for nothing, and this doesn't happen anywhere in the world. It took thousands of years of enslavement and punishment before the Hebrews were willing to give up false gods, and accept the God we worship today, and the Black race will not achieve equality by any way but by earning the respect for their good works, and not their evil.

The destruction of Christian and Godly ethics is then on the agenda of the Socialist movement, and this is just another step toward New World Order, wherein is only the secular belief.

This is an important segment of the plan to force America to accept rule by a foreign power. It is though, within the Christian and Judaic religion is the belief during this time of temptation, when the United States of America and Israel are flirting and even whoring after the powers being formed in Europe today, God will step in and keep us in this hour of temptation, according to the promise of the Scriptures. His final warning Revelation 3:11, "Behold, I come quickly; hold that fast which thou hast, that no man may take thy crown.

This has been an insight into what is happening in the Christian nations, how they are seemingly pulling apart in such actions as Quebec in Canada wishing to be its own nation within a nation, but allied with France, and similar actions around the world. As the earth enters the end time, there are actions occurring in heaven that has certain repercussions here on earth, and one of the first is Christ opening the seals of the book of life. There are seven seals and each seal brings a different event to reality on earth.

Revelation 6:2, The first seal is opened, "And I saw and behold a white horse: and he that sat on him had a bow: and a crown was given unto him: and he went forth conquering and to conquer. This is the Caucasian Christian nations arising out of the twelve tribes of Israel, bringing forth the Christian movement throughout the world. This is in concert with what Christ reveals in Matthew 24:14, "And this gospel of the kingdom shall be preached in all the world for a witness unto all nations: and then shall the end come. From the day Christ sent his first disciples into the world as missionaries, the word of God has been spread throughout the world. In today's world, with the advent of radio and television, and through missionaries, there are few spots left on earth where the coming kingdom has not been preached. The distribution of the Holy Bible, and other printed material notifying the world of the end time and of Christ's return has also been widely distributed. The proclamation and effort is not producing sizable returns, because of the entrenchment of Islamic, eastern religions, and cults such as devil worship, and atheism. This time is preparatory to having God's servants sealed as described in Revelation 7.

The second seal is open, and we read in Revelation 6:4 "And there went out another horse that was red: and power was given to him to him that sat thereon to take peace from the earth, and that they should kill one another: and there was a great sword given unto him. This descr ibes the socialist government arising in Europe today, and the Communist movement now centered in China. The socialist movement is the movement expanding in the United States and other Christian nations under the disguise of being the government of choice by the people, and its growth is documented by the slim margins in which the year 2000 election was won by the conservative candidate over the liberal candidate. Although voter turnout was higher than most elections, there is great apathy generated because of several major causes. First, the silent majority, the overall population did not have a candidate they felt would represent them. These people felt left out of the voting because to them it was a question of voting for virtually the same thing, because there are few differences between the way the nation would be governed under either administration.

To most it was to vote for the weak or weaker, and they just weren't interested. Both political parties in the United States are very adamant in keeping any other party from gaining any sizable following, and this is in part possible because of the media coverage, and the two parties have exposure to the public, but where very little coverage is afforded the other political parties in the United States. It is recognized by the knowing, that the media controls what is to reach the public, and that information is selectively slanted to achieve what the media wishes to use to supplement their own agenda.

The population of the nation is thereby denied the absolute truth about the news, about the candidates, and about the issues. This is quite noticeable wherein after major speeches, supposed news experts and analysts are interviewed after the speech, to inform the general public what the person making the speech actually said, instead of what the public heard. It is based on the idea that most people are literally too dumb to understand what the speaker said, so the speech has to be analyzed and the (truth?) real meaning made clear. Surely even looking at the advertising put forth on the media gives the idea that each individual is believed to be too stupid to live life unless they follow the advice of the experts. This is in evidence that a doctor has to tell you which brand of aspirin to use for your headache, or medicine for your hemorrhoids, or toothpaste to use for brushing your teeth. What's wrong with this is people are getting used to being told by supposed experts what to do, what to think, and what to believe, and this is just as true when it comes to understanding God's word also. Believe, there is no requirement for someone to interpret the Holy Bible for you, because as you read, the Holy Ghost will adapt your thinking to the message God wishes you to have. Can it not be recognized by the constant pounding of rhetoric, people become adapted to letting others decide for them, what to eat, buy, believe, and do? Isn't that enslavement of the mind and body? If you cannot live, if you cannot believe, and if you cannot act independently, then you are enslaved to whatever system there is.

The socialist system is only slightly removed from the communist system, and in the coming government in Europe they will both be well represented, and under this coming government, an individual will be no better than a worker bee, ant or termite, or any other socialized insect. It's time for each person to seriously think about this, and act accordingly.

A look at the communist (the red horse) is to look at Communist China today, and these things are in the near future. The return of the two major cities by the western powers of the world to China, has given China a financial base to support her atheist belief, and to further her world conquest goals. The huge population of China is sufficient to maintain the largest armed force in the world, and with the west legally and illegally supplying the needed technology for better weapon systems, and military applications, China is ready to become more aggressive in the world to assert her domination. The major sea lanes of the world is under communist China's control, or in affiliation with countries friendly to communist China, and this impact is going to be felt just shortly as China makes a bid for world conquest. The next step of China is to acquire Taiwan and the other islands near the coast, and China has already said she is about to claim all territory and people within 2000 miles of her coastline, and this is to reach to the Philippine islands. A look at the fact that China, with her population has to either have even stricter birth control, or more land for the coming generations, and there has to be a way to feed, and clothe this additional population. Expansion of her borders is the only way this is possible, and that means military take over and war.

There are two possibilities as to the great sword China has as the red horse. The first is her huge population, being able to supply manpower into the armed forces in greater number than the rest of the world put together, and maintaining it for many years more than any nation or combination of nations.

The second possibility is that China has the atomic weapons, and is improving her rocket systems where they will rival Russia's and the United States capability. There is concern that Russia will join China militarily, but from the Scriptures it seems more likely that Russia is to become involved in the government forming in Europe, which is going to concede control to China. Two powers on the earth today have now been described in the white horse and the red horse, with the third horse to come into existence. Revelation 6:5, "And when he had opened the third seal, I heard the third beast say, Come and see. And I beheld, and lo, a black horse: and he that sat on him had a pair of balances in his hand. This is the emergence of the black nations of Africa, and we see this power just beginning to take shape. The apartheid government has been cast out, and black rule is being established. Right now the Islamic forces are busy trying to convert these people to the Islamic faith, and soon China is going to entice them toward communism by expanded trade. It has to be remembered that China needs space and raw materials, and Africa is a heartland for both. The western capitalist nations (supposedly the Christian nations) are going to tinker around in Africa with token support, but having had to abandon the colonial power once exerted in Africa, the land will be written off as too costly to pursue further.

This puts Africa, and its black population, as a deciding factor in world power, and which ever way these people go, the world will go, and it isn't going to be toward Christianity and the capitalistic type government. The mention of food grains, oil, and wine indicates there is to develop a trade, and it can be supposed this is going to come between China and the black nations. The emerging nations are in terrible shape for trying to feed the people, and there isn't enough capital in the nations to pay for food from the western nations. China needs raw material and space, and Africa offers both, and this means China can make good inroads by giving aid, and trading with the new nations of Africa.

Is there anyway to change the outcome of what the Scriptures say? The answer is no, and the Christian is to just watch as these events unfold.

The last power that is to come on earth before we enter into the end time is another forming power and it's center is located in Iraq. We read of this power in Revelation 6:8, "And I looked and behold a pale horse: and his name that sat on him was Death, and Hell followed with him. And power was given unto them over the fourth part of the earth, to kill with the sword, and with hunger, and with death, and with beasts of the earth.

Not too many take seriously this power that is currently situated in Iraq, but it is soon to rise to higher world prominence. Look at the events that have occurred. This year 2001, marks the tenth anniversary where the United States ousted Iraq from Kuwait, and since that time has tried to contain Iraq. Despite the effort of the United nations, the United States, and Britain, Iraq continues to deny United Nations inspection of the manufacturing plants for nuclear, biological, and chemical warfare weapons.

The sanctions put on the nation is becoming like a sieve, where vital materials are flowing in from China, Arabia, and other nations in violation to the installed sanctions, and nothing is being done about these violations. In fact, in the near future, the sanctions will be relaxed by the United States, and other nations, because of Saudi Arabia, and other Arab nations protests of keeping the sanctions in place. The result is going to be that a coalition of Arab states is going to form with Iraq, the old Babylon, as the leader, and this sets up the conditions for Revelation 17:5 to occur. "And upon her forehead was a name written, MYSTERY BABYLON THE MOTHER OF HARLOTS AND ABOMINATIONS OF THE EARTH. The coalition of Arab nations will have the ability to cripple the economies of the nations such as America, who are heavily dependent on Arab oil for industry. The United States, even withdrawing its exports of oil to other nations, could not supply the American need for oil, and without an alternate source or an alternate way to conduct everyday use, the United States would virtually come to a halt as the supply dwindles. This would become exceptionally critical if oil had to used by the military to check the spread of communism by China at the same time, and to intervene in Israel because of the threat there. You know what? Neither of these things is going to get done because of the Arab coalition. Iraq will succeed in capturing Israel, and this is written in Revelation 16:19, "And the great city was divided into three parts, and the cities of the nations fell: and the great Babylon came in remembrance before God, to give unto her the cup of wine of the fierceness of his wrath.

Current negotiations about Jerusalem are going on right now, and the past history of this great city has to be looked at. In the past the city had four quarters, the Jewish, the Armenian, the Moslem, and the Christian, but as of late, they are talking about three sectors, the Islamic or Moslem, the Judaic or Jewish sector, and the Christian sector. By what is revealed in the Holy

189

Bible this is to be the accord agreed upon just shortly.

What happens then is revealed by what Christ tells us in Matthew 24:15, "When ye therefore shall see the abomination of desolation, spoken of by Daniel the prophet, stand in the holy place, (whoso readeth, let him understand.) What Daniel said of this time starts in Daniel 9:25, "Know therefore and understand, that from the going forth of the commandment to restore and to build Jerusalem unto the Messiah the Prince shall be seven weeks, and three score and two weeks: the street shall be built again, and the wall, even in troublous time. There are plans to get Jerusalem rebuilt, and this gives the time table for that reconstruction, so with this in mind, despite the big hassle over the city that is going on, the city, its streets and wall will be restored, and divided into three sectors by the peace agreement. There can only this be said about this event. When it happens, watch out!

Daniel continues in verse 27, "And he shall confirm the covenant with many for one week: and in the midst of the week he shall cause the sacrifice and the oblation to cease, and for the over spreading of abominations he shall make it desolate, even unto the consummation, and that determined shall be poured upon the desolate.

The invading power, Iraq representing the Arab coalition of nations, will tell the world they accept the terms of the division of the city, then in the middle of the next week he invades the city, takes away the daily Jewish worship, and installs the Islamic code, which means no Jew will go to the temple even unto the end time. The abomination is the installing of the Islamic code in the Jewish temple, and the desolation is the inability for the Jews to carry out their daily worship of God. This is further explained in Daniel 11:31, "And arms shall stand on his part, and they shall pollute the sanctuary of strength, and shall take away the daily sacrifice, and they shall place the abomination that maketh desolate.

The armed forces (arms) shall take over the Jewish temple (which is the sanctuary of strength of the Jews) and shall take away the daily sacrifice (worship service) and shall place the abomination (the Islamic worship service) in the temple, wherein no Jew will attend, and being cut off from their religious worship, are desolate.

What is to happen next is written in Daniel 12:11, "And from the time that the daily sacrifice shall be taken away, and the abomination that maketh desolate is set up, there shall be a thousand two hundred and ninety days. This is about three and a half years to the end time. We are then given a time table of events of the world conditions leading into the end time, and these milestones are passing one by one, almost daily, and this is to make Christ's prophecy in Matthew 24:22 be true. "And except those days be shortened, there should no flesh be saved: but for the elect's sake those days will be shortened. This means these events are going to start occurring in rapid fire succession, so the end time will pass quickly, otherwise no person would be saved.

Look at what is going on in the world today. The Christian nations are beginning to falter, the secular government is Europe is coming into power, Israel is about to make peace with the Palestinians, and live to regret it, China is starting to make a bid for world conquest, and the African nations are trying to get some kind of a toe hold in the world for survival. And the ancient Babylon (Iraq) is making a bid for power in the mid east.

The four major powers are on earth and getting in to position, and during this somewhat lull on earth, Revelation 6:9, 10, and 11, is taking place in heaven.

Now in Revelation 6:12, the sixth seal is opened, and for the first time, we have a physical event occurring on earth that is to announce the beginning of the end time that we can recognize for sure as being the end time. "And I beheld when he had opened the sixth seal, and, lo, there was a great earthquake; and the sun became black as sackcloth of hair, and the moon became as blood. This event is going to be a catastrophic event involving the whole world, and it is probably going to be the result of the extraction of the oil and minerals from deep in the earth, and leaving the voids to collapse under the compression of gravity. When this event occurs, enough debris in the form of dust is going to blot out the sun, and the moon will look as red as blood. To get a idea of this take a piece of glass and darken it with black smoke, and then look at the moon through it. The moon will appear red. The only reason we'll see the moon is that it is 230,000 miles from the earth, as compared to the sun at ninety three million miles from earth.

It can't be over stressed that if man were cautious, more sane use and exploitation of the earth would be in practice today, but this isn't going to occur, so man must suffer the consequences of his greed and actions. Those realizing the truth have to stand by and await for these first indications to pass, and the sealing of those to be saved is started. At this time a person needs to pray that he be included in those saved.

In Revelation 6:12 was the great earthquake, and now in verse 13, "And the stars of heaven fell upon the earth, even as a fig tree casteth her untimely figs, when she is shaken of a mighty wind. This event is going to be a meteor or asteroid shower that starts as a single large body that breaks up as it strikes earth's atmosphere, but is big enough to roar into the earth shaking it mightily. This is exactly what the scientists today fear is about to happen, and apparently this is going to occur before science can come up with a solution to prevent it. Right today they are tracking, and trying to discover any bodies that might be a threat to earth, and the catalogue is getting thicker every day, as the changing orbits of these potentially dangerous objects are plotted. The thinking is that some plan, whether it be destroying the invading body, or deflecting the body, has to be established and ready for use in the very near future.

When this giant body goes screaming through earth's atmosphere, the shock wave and the heat wave is going to tear earth's atmosphere apart, and as it says in Revelation 6:14, "And the heaven departed as a scroll when it is rolled together; and every mountain and island was moved out of its place. The object going through the atmosphere pushes it apart with the shock and heat waves, but that creates a void in its trail, where the atmosphere is going to close like the two ends of a scroll suddenly rolling inward until they are together. At nearly the same time, the object collides with earth, and every island and mountain is moved out of position as the result of tectonic plate movement. The earth is molten in the center, and this gives it some pliability, so as the object smacks into the planet on one side, it bulges on the opposite side, then returns to as it was before. This means every piece of land is affected by this movement.

It is at this time people on earth realize the end time is upon them, and head for the mountains as a hope to escape the coming disasters. Revelation 6:16 and 17 gives voice to what the people on earth are going to utter when this happens. "And said to the mountains and rocks, Fall on us, and hide us from the face of him that sitteth upon the throne, and from the wrath of the Lamb. For the great day of his wrath is come; and who shall be able to stand?

After this collision and the great turmoil on earth has subsided, the atmosphere has settled down, and a great calm settles over earth, and this is when the sealing takes place. In this relatively calm, people are going to believe the worst is over and begin to live life again according to their traditions, but the wise are going to know this is only temporary respite, and more is to come, so these people pick up the Christian religion knowing the end is come, and Christ is the Savior.

Out of the twelve tribes of Israel, those dedicated to the Judaic faith, there are only 144,000 sealed and of all the Jews that has lived, this is but a token amount, and that means if the Jews are to be preserved it must take place within the confines of conversion to the Christian faith. In Revelation 7:9, is recorded, "After this I beheld, and, lo, a great multitude which no man could number, of all nations, and kindreds, and people, and tongues, stood before the throne, and before the Lamb, clothed in white robes with palms in their hands. These are the Christians of the world, and they are explained in verse 14, "And I said unto him, Sir, thou knowest. And he said unto me, These are they which came out of the great tribulation; and have washed their robes, and made them white in the blood of the Lamb. The great tribulation has to occur sometime after the rebuilding of the temple, roads and wall in Jerusalem, and the implementation of the abomination that makes desolate, and before the sealing of the multitude. This is prophesied by Christ in Matthew 24:21, speaking after the fall of Jerusalem, "For then shall be a great tribulation, such as was not since the beginning of the world to this time, no, nor ever shall be.

What is this tribulation? Chapter 12 of Revelation deals with the birth of Christ and the expulsion of Satan from heaven, and the establishment that he is on earth and in power. We know this occurred about 2000 years ago, and so the beginning of Revelation 13:1 applies to sometime after Christ's death, and up to this time in the history of man, not all of the powers on earth were in known presence as they are today.

The Arab nations, prior to oil being discovered there, were of little importance in world affairs, but are now very influential. The African nations under the control of colonial powers were insignificant in world affairs but are now making their entrance into the world as the black horseman, and holding the set of balances in his hand. Communism didn't really get started until the beginning of the twentieth century, and is still growing under the combined force of socialism. Christianity has only been on the face of the earth for two thousand years, so powers represented by the four horsemen only arrived on earth within the past century. With these four powers either established or coming in to prominence in the world, the time is ripe for the tribulation to come about, and it is in the form of the socialist government that is rising in Europe today. Here is where the deception comes in. The government that is to rise out of Europe is going to be one based on financial, probably in the stock markets and other world wide financial activity, including the world bank. This will appear as a capitalistic system, but it's going to be a sham, and just about every nation in the world is going to be taken in by this government's deceit.

Here's the description of it in Revelation 13: 1, "And I stood upon the sand of the sea, and I saw a beast rise up out of the sea, having seven heads and ten horns, and upon his horns ten crowns, and upon his heads the name of blasphemy. The seven heads are going to be the seven principle nations that are going to build the pact in the European Community, and it is going to surprise many about what occurs. It says in verse 2, the beast is like a leopard, and the leopard is consistent with the Arab nations of the world. This means the Arab, (oil producing nations) are going to play a vital part in the community of nations forming in Europe today, and under the leadership of Germany. This makes sense since the manufacturing ability of Europe depends heavily on oil today, and as the manufacturing increases (which it is today) more oil will have to be diverted from non producers, and lower priced fuel users, such as the United States, to be sold to the higher paying nations in Europe. The leopard, (the oil producers in the Arab nations) are then going to be the body, or foundation of the government in Europe. This means the government of Europe will be greatly influenced by the Arab nations because of their reliance on oil.

This government has feet like the bear, and the bear represents Russia becoming the nation in which strength is given to shore up that government. At present NATO, the North Atlantic Treaty Organization, serves as the arm of Europe for military, and Europe is reliant on America for men, equipment, and money to maintain this armed force for the protection of nations in the alliance. This is to soon be converted over to a United Nations force, under the control of Germany, and with this conversion, Russia can supply the needed armament, technology, and manpower to Europe, creating the second largest uniformed army in the world. China will be the biggest armed forces nation in the world, and the combined forces of Europe and Russia will be the second largest.

This puts the western powers into a almost isolation status, too small to compete with the bigger armed forces that are to soon develop.

When it says in verse 2, "... and his mouth was as the mouth of a lion .... is to show England's part in this government, and is more of a voice (the mouth) rather than an integral operating part of the government. This is representative right now, as how England in its usually conservative way, plays some part of the role in European affairs, but for the large part is steering clear of too deep involvement. This is more favorable to the United States at this time, because what is occurring in the world is nation after nation is succumbing to the pressure of having to deal and trade with Europe, and are gradually coming under the control of the European government. This is further explained by Revelation 13:3, "And one of its heads as it were wounded to death; and his deadly wound was healed: and all the world wondered after the beast. This is Germany, and it can be understood, by knowing that Germany has come to being a world power three times and has failed thee times, with every one in the world believing that when Nazi Germany was defeated, it ended Germany's ability to ever rise to power again. Here again Germany has fooled the world, because since the end of WWII, she has become stronger than most of the nations in the world, a remarkable feat for a nation only two thirds the size of Texas in America.

Go back now to the end part of verse 2 , "...and the dragon gave him his power, and his seat, and his great authority. This is a pact between the European Community under the charter of the United Nations, and led by Germany, and with communist China, a non aggression pact, similar to what occurred between the USSR and The United States of America. When these two countries were the super powers of the world, they understood that a conflict between them could serve no useful purpose, because while they might lay each other to waste, neither would survive to reap the harvest.

With the first and second largest armed forces in the world, that of China and the European Community of nations (probably to be called the United Nations of Europe) close to each other, war would only prove beneficial to the United States, Canada, Australia, and other Christian nations that have not given themselves over to Europe. This is why the pact comes about and leaves the nations of the world to wonder the question asked in verse 4, "Who is like unto the beast? Who is able to make war with him?

Consider the great powers on earth at this time. There is the Arab coalition of nations under the leadership of Iraq (to fill the prophecy of Babylon the great). There are the United Nations of Europe under the leadership of Germany (a nation thought to have died in being a world power in WWII) but is again rising to power toda. There is the dragon of the world, China, which is to have the largest armed forces in the world. There are the emerging black nations of Africa that will be the deciding factor in which way the world's government will go, and there are the remaining Christian nations of the world that will huddle together against the combined might of the other three.

Take a look at what happens next. This financially based government is only going to last forty two months, but it is enough time for this government under German control, and with the support of China, and the coalition of Arab nations to fulfill the prophecy in Revelation 13:7, "And it was given unto him to make war with the saints, and to overcome them: and power was given him over all kindreds, and tongues, and nations. This is the defeat of America, and all the other Christian nations (the saints) in the world. However, the expenditures required to accomplish this breaks the financial economy of the government in Europe, and out of this collapse comes a new beast government.

This government is described in Revelation 13:11, "And I beheld another beast coming up out of the earth; and he had two horns like a lamb, and he spake as a dragon. Out of the rubble of the Europe's financial-based government arises a socialist and scientific-oriented and shared power regime. This is the meaning of the two horns like a lamb, and the socialist approach to enslaving the world is not as harsh as the communist way, so communism is out and socialism is in, and science that is the second part of the new government speaks as loud as the Chinese dragon had spoken in the fallen government. "And he exerciseth all the power of the first beast before him, and causeth the earth and them which dwell therein to worship the first beast, whose deadly wound was healed. Here again, Germany comes to the front, still in charge and worshipped by those who are charmed by her ability to continue on after so many failures. Here is where science comes into the picture as a controlling partner, it is found in Revelation 13:13, "And he doeth great wonders, so that he maketh fire come down from heaven on the earth in the sight of men. This probably indicates the United States will build a missile defense system in outer space and these missiles, or weapons, will come under the control of this government in Europe to be used as a hedge against any nation wanting to make war against the seated government of the world.

The first part of the time of the great tribulation is come, now return to the events after the sealing of the nations of people. Now the seventh seal is opened, and we read this in Revelation 8: 1, "And when he had opened the seventh seal there was a silence in heaven about the space of half an hour. This is a peaceful time on earth, and can be related to what happens when seven angels get ready to blow their trumpets, heralding more catastrophes on earth, still part of the great tribulation. Another angel, above the seven, takes a censer of fire from God's altar, and casts it to earth, and this is indicative of what is said in Revelation 13:13, where the government, to deceive the inhabitants of the earth, puts on a fire display to convince the earth, they, and not God, were the ones to bring down the fire from heaven.

This is in keeping what Christ prophesied in Matthew 24:24, "For there shall arise false Christs, and false prophets, and shall shew great signs and wonders; inasmuch that if it were possible, they will deceive the very elect. How this is done is in Revelation 13:14, "And deceiveth them that dwell on the earth by the means of these miracles which he had power to do in the sight of the beast; saying to them that dwell on the earth; that they should make a image to the beast, which had the wound by a sword and did live. And he had power to give life unto the image of the beast, that the image of the beast should both speak and cause as many as would not worship the image of the beast should be killed.

The head of the government in Europe is going to be a cloned man, and even though he is wounded in a battle, he lives through it, and as the leader, he has another man cloned from him, which is in his image, to inherit the kingdom the first has set up. The reason the Holy Bible refers to them as beasts, is because they do not have the Spirit of God dwelling in them, and are therefore the same as animals. This is something science hasn't taken into account about the cloning of people. This leader, the cloned man, tries to pass off this cloned image as a Christ, and those who refuse to worship this image are slain. Many are going to be deceived by this, as stated in Matthew 24:24. "For there shall arise false Christs, and false prophets, and shall show great signs and wonders; insomuch that, they shall deceive the very elect.

Although there have been several men referring to themselves as gods and Christs, these men are part of the deceivers, and as the earth enters this end time, these are going to become more pronounced as cloning and other means of copying people occur. A person shouldn't be surprised that the technologies in science can be developed to use living cells to clone another being, because the formula for life was laid out at the beginning of time when God himself formed, and created the first life. It is man's direction which is wrong, and for which man is to pay heavily for as he approaches the end time. This behavior is dangerous enough to say Stop! Look! and Listen! or at least look before you leap! but it is doubtful man will look at being reasonable, he been deceived too much already. The hope lies in the individual, and it's going to be each individual's actions and belief which is going to determine his end. That can't be over stressed.

In Thessalonians 2:3, "Let no man deceive you by any means: for that day shall not come, except there come a falling away first, and that man of sin be revealed the son of perdition. Despite this warning, man is going to be deceived, as a general body, but some individuals will stay staunchly with God and Christ. Pray that you are among them.

Under this dominating socialist world, Revelation 13:16 comes into being. "And he causeth all, both small and great, rich and poor, free and bond, to receive a mark in their right hand or in their forehead.

This mark is going to be installed chips such as is used today to identify pets and livestock, only it will be imprinted with what rights is granted to the individual, and by the Scriptures there are four levels. There are those with the mark in their forehead, which are probably the lowest in the society, then those with the mark in their right hand, then above those the people who have the name of the beast, and last those who have the number of the beast. However the marking, there is to be the workers, then perhaps the soldiers, then the managers, and lastly the close in associates, the overall managers, and then the beast himself. The number 666 has always remained a mystery as to the meaning, but it can be guessed it will be something like the 666 the cloned person, or the 666 person cloned in descending genetic line. It may even be something as simple as the Petrie dish from which the man was cloned, (i.e. experiment 666.)

The technology for doing this is already in use, and it will be like using your credit debit card when you purchase groceries, or other such necessities. The scanner will decide if you can get the requested goods or not, and it can be suspected that as many people as will be on earth, and with the things happening, there will not be sufficient food and materials for people. Similar to the crisis in Russia trying to rebuild today, or the rebuilding of Japan and Germany after WWII

This puts earth into the time when the world is basically under one rule, but not necessarily out. To get the whole picture we have to go back to Revelation 8:7. It has to be remembered that when God sends fire raining down on earth, as the angel throws the fire from the censer, that the government is going to say they did it, and use stored missiles or some device in orbit as a means of deceiving people into believing the government did do it. Now God sends another sign, and this is going to be

201

really evident, because it concerns the space station that is being put in space today, or a later model of it.

"The first angel sounded, and there followed hail and fire mingled with blood, and they were cast upon the earth: and the third part of trees were burned up, and all the green grass was burnt up. The only thing near earth today that can cause this effect is the space station, and it appears that for some reason the station is going to fail and come crashing back to earth. The hail is caused by the gasses and water vapor in the station as it plummets through the atmosphere, and of course it will be fiery as in the Challenger disaster, and there must be a significant amount of life aboard for their blood to be mixed fire and hail. As it crashes onto earth, the chemicals released destroys a third of the remaining forests in the world, and that places it, (giving the logging that is going on around the equator) somewhere in the northern latitudes, where it is too expensive to log. This means somewhere in places like Russia, Alaska or Canada. This loss is going to occur probably for several reasonable reasons, and they need to be looked at. The world has just come out of a war, and there is nothing available to effect a rescue. Then too, as the war starts, and the government of the free nations realize it is a lost cause, some of them may crowd into the space station in the belief they will be safe, until they can return to earth, and set up a rebellion. This would account of why there would be a lot of people aboard the station.

Revelation 8:8, "And the second angel sounded, and as if it were a great mountain burning with fire was cast into the sea: and the third part of the sea became blood: And the third part of the creatures which were in the sea, and had life died; and the third part of the ships were destroyed.

This is evidently the main part of the station housing the majority of people, and when it is realized the station is failing, (too late for the arm of the station) the ships are sent to effect a possible rescue of any survivors, and destroyed in the process.

Because of the sequence of the events, it has to be looked at that this event is indicative of a failing Universe, and that gravity is causing the Universe to collapse back in on itself. In Revelation 10 and 11, a great asteroid or comet smashes into earth, and its impact really raises havoc. It pollutes a third of the fresh water on earth, and people drinking the polluted water die. In Revelation 8:12, "And the fourth angel sounded and the third part of the sun was smitten, and the third part of the moon, and the third part of the stars; so as the third part of them were darkened, and the day shone not for the third part of it, and the night likewise. The earth's day is based upon the rotation of earth on its axis, and to shorten both the day and night, the planet's rotational speed has to be increased, and that evidently is the aftermath of the asteroid or comet smashing into earth, at an angle that increases its rotational speed. There can not be any doubt in any person's mind that the earth is in its death throes, and doesn't have long to survive, but it still doesn't sink in to the majority, because they have been so badly deceived by science, education, government, and commerce. Society on earth is no different from that of the social insects.

In Revelation 9: 1, we read, "And the fifth angel sounded, and I saw an angel fall from heaven unto the earth: and to him was given the key of the bottomless pit. And he opened the bottomless pit; and there arose a smoke out of the pit, as the smoke of a great furnace; and the sun and the air were darkened by the reason of the smoke of the pit.

Here comes the coalition of Arab nations under the leadership of Iraq (Babylon) where they break away from the socialist government of Europe, and this happens because they finally have exploded a bomb that is equal to an erupting volcano on earth, a truly massive weapon that reaches deep into the earth. Armed with this horrendous weapon, and the armaments shortly to be described, the nations ready themselves for the last war on earth.

It has to be remembered that John is describing in common terms of the day what he is seeing in heaven. If for instance, you had been an eye witness to the first atomic explosion, how would you describe it? Most report the familiar mushroom cloud, the fire, and the shock wave, and we understand this because it is familiar language to us, so John is trying to say what he saw, by using familiar words of that day. Locusts were a common sight in those days, and they are compared to the modern day helicopter. A dragon fly was used as the model for the first helicopter, and they have progressed considerably since that time. In reading Revelation 9:3 through 10, keep in mind a fleet of helicopters launched by Babylon and associate nations, against the government in Europe. "And there came out of the smoke locusts upon the earth; and unto them was given power as scorpions of the earth have power. The sting of a scorpion is very painful, and disabling for awhile, but seldom fatal. This fleet of helicopters are armed with some type of chemical or biological weapon that disables a person five months. Think about the rudimentary plans of war. If you kill a person outright, you only have to bury them, and this requires one or two people for a few hours, but if you injure a person, rehabilitation requires several people for long periods of time, and is much more costly.

"And it was commanded them that they should not hurt the grass of the earth, neither any green thing, neither any tree; but only those men which have not the seal of God in their foreheads. The Islamic nations are still out to install the Islamic faith throughout the world. The Christians of the world have been pretty well wiped out, so the two major forces are the Islamic forces, and the secular forces. Whatever bacteria or chemical is used is harmless to vegetation, and that puts it into being something like a virus or bacteria that affects only man. "And it was given that they should not kill them, but that they should be tormented for five months: and their torment was as the torment of a scorpion when he striketh man. And in those days shall men seek death, and shall not find it; and shall desire to die; and death shall flee from them.

In Revelation 9:7, is the description that pretty accurately describes a helicopter, which is now the choice of weapon for battlefield support. "And the shapes of the locusts were like horses prepared unto battle, their heads were as it were crowns like gold: and their faces were as the faces of men. A person viewing a helicopter operating close to the ground, sees the pilot quite clearly, and they do wear helmets, and these helmets are painted gold color. In verse 8 is written, "And they had hair as the hair of women, and their teeth were as the teeth of lions. And they had breastplates, as it were breastplates of iron; and the sound of their wings was as the sound of chariots of many horses running to battle. It's not hard to imagine this is the description of the rotary wings (the turning of the rotor) and making its loud wop-wopping sound which makes a pretty good racket, as opposed to a jet airplane, or other war vehicle. The fact the pilots wear long hair, the traditional fashion today, may indicate this as being the hair style of the future, or it may indicate we are closer to this time than we think. They have the teeth of lions which means the front end of the chopper is armed with destructive weapons like the machine gun that shreds flesh as if torn by a lion. Then in verse 10, "And they had tails like unto scorpions, and there were stings in their tails: and their power was to hurt men five months. The long slender tail of a scorpion is like a helicopter's tail section, and armed back there is the biological or chemical dispensing boom, or stinger.

A helicopter flying over a battle field dispensing a biological or bacterial spray, would be a very effective weapon, at a fairly low cost. This is exactly what Iraq is working on this very day, and why the United States and the United Nations are trying to stymie the production of these weapons by Iraq.

In opposition to Iraq comes an army of millions of men, (200,000,000), and they have different weapons. These weapons must be like the modern day tank, and we read about them in Revelation 9:17. "And thus I saw the horses in the vision, and them that sat on them, having breastplates of fire, and of jacinth, and brimstone: and the heads of the horse were as heads of lions; and out of their mouths issued fire and smoke and brimstone. These are evidently tank like vehicles armed with laser type weapons, which are being perfected today. The fire, smoke and brimstone indicates a high heat weapon, capable of melting the sand and earth, and that power is confined to atomic and laser weapons. These weapons, mounted on the front of the vehicle is a very withering fire in slaying men, and like the helicopter used by the other side, these vehicles have a biological or chemical dispenser in the rear, that also disables men. "For their power their mouth, and in their tails: for their tails were like unto serpents, and had heads, and with them they do hurt. The outcome of this war is recorded in Revelation 18:2, "And he cried mightily with a strong voice, saying Babylon the great is fallen, and is become the habitation of devils, and hold of every foul spirit, and the cage of unclean and hateful bird. This is as far as will be gone into the end time, because the mystery is mostly solved, and it remains up to each individual to choose which way to live in life, and whether or not they will be lifted from the woes that is shortly to come upon earth.

The best advice that can be given is recorded in Philippians 4:8, "Finally, brethren, whatsoever things that are true, whatsoever things are honest, whatsoever things are just, whatsoever things are pure, whatsoever things are lovely, whatsoever things are of good report; if there be any virtue, and if there be any praise, think on these things.

CHAPTER 8

A New Life

Those who manage to get through temptation and those who avoid being destroyed in the lake of fire are to witness the most fantastic of miracles. It begins in Revelation 2 1: 1, "And I saw a new heaven and a new earth: for the first heaven and the first earth were passed away; and there was no more sea. This rebuilding of the heaven and earth is the climax of God's great endeavor to create a unique being called man, which is in the image and likeness of himself, and to have him habituate the planet earth as little Gods, and having immortality, and being without sin or violence. The city of Jerusalem on earth today is to be the spot on earth where the New Jerusalem is to be located in this very final time, and a person need read Revelation 22 in order to understand what the conditions will be like in those days.

Meanwhile, what is there that a person can do to insure they are to be among those to survive the calamities and be with God and Christ for ever and ever? It's actually a very simple format.

God laid out ten commandments to follow for having a successful physical and spiritual life. Christ came along and demonstrated how a person can life that life, and gain immortality through being perfect before God's eyes. And lastly, God has seen to it that we have received his word in the Holy Bible as a handbook for living life on earth physically, and prepare ourselves spiritually for the life afterward. What more could a person ask for in guidance? There's an old saying in the world and it is very appropriate here, "If it ain't in the book, don't do it! "

It has to be stressed again that an individual has to read and absorb what the Holy Bible tells about life, and the person has to have an open enough mind to let the Holy Ghost come in and work in the person's mind. Your minister may reflect his observations about life, as any person can, but it has to be reconciled as to whether or not it is in accordance with what God, Christ, and the Holy Ghost has put before you. Interpretation should lay toward acceptance of what the Holy Ghost reveals and not what friends, relatives, and neighbors say. No man can give you as accurate information as God, and no man can act as your Savior. You aren't going to be able to stand before God and say, "So and so told me this is the way....

In other things, each person can afford to give fifteen minutes out of the day to read and reflect on what is read in the Holy Bible, and then follow the lesson learned. No major changes are going to be effected immediately, unless the person desires such change, but over a period of time, the small changes you make through acceptance of God's truth begins to exert changes that may offend those who are lost, but which insures you are rewarded by God.

It is entirely true that what the citizens of a nation believes, and how they act determines the state of the nation's health. The free nations of the world, if they wish to remain free, have to have each individual's participation in government, education, and commerce. If God fearing, God and Christ led men and women are elected into government leadership positions, then the nation will be under God, and prosperity will result.

It is as Christ says in Matthew 24, "Make sure that no man deceives you. and this is especially true when dealing with politicians and organizations, or people in general. There is no such thing as a good crook, and there is no such thing as an ornery God. What we sow we also reap, and that is true in politics, or in life.

The imagined spoof of a separation between church and state is just that, all spoof, because as people believe, so goes the nation. There are only two beliefs in the world. Either there is a God, in which the prudent will adhere to his guidance, or there is the belief that no God exists, and therefore man can live according to his supposed animal instincts. Civility, good manners, good ethics, good behavior, fearlessness, and prosperity are the marks of a nation under God. Strife, confusion, ill behavior, fear, doubt, anxiety, poor ethics, and failure are the marks and reward for those who are secular.

What is strange is that people want all the good things that come from a belief in God, but they do not want to accept God, nor do his bidding, and this bit of nonsense comes from the over inflated egos of modem man. You cannot serve God, and man, but in serving God you also serve man, whereas; if you serve man, you may not be serving God.

While it is entirely true that God has had to continually adjust his plan, because of man's instability, i.e. Eve eating of the forbidden fruit, it doesn't mean that God is ready to abandon man entirely. When God destroyed all life on earth, he spared Noah, and his family, so the world would be replenished with mankind, all related and which should have lived in peace and harmony, but man, under Satan's influence fails to recognize the lessons God wishes him to learn. As earth enters into the last days, some will be lifted up to serve as Noah and his son's, as seed for the world to come.

Those who are prudent, those who are wise, and those who are practical will make sure they are among the ones that will be on this last Noah's ark, for this is the last boat, and those left behind will be like those left ashore when Noah sailed.

In this modem day, rational thinking in the terms of religion, has come to a all time low, and the words of man is taken far better than is the word of God. It is difficult for any person to cope with the mass of information designed to lead a person away from God and Christ, and toward the ultimate destruction that awaits those refusing to accept God as the Supreme power and being. About the only recourse a person has is to separate away from the world spiritually, and quietly maintain his alliance with God and Christ on a one to one basis. The time is shortly coming when father and son, mother and daughter can no longer abide in each other, and this is becoming more prevalent every day, as evidenced by the children in their early teens running away to be on their own.

What is the answer? What man should be striving to do is to recreate the alliance between God and man, and that means a radical shift in man's thinking, and the installation of Godly values. Unfortunately, this is not to come to pass until Christ returns and takes the planet and people away from Satan. The true Christians are the only people in the world who are going to ask fervently for the return of Christ to earth. The others wish to prolong their imagined luxury and evil doings to the last moment. The advice to the Christian is written in Colossians 3:17, "And whatsoever ye do in word or deed, do all in the name of the Lord Jesus, giving thanks to God and the Father by him.

In consideration that the earth and man are about to enter the end time, it is both prudent and practical to review the code of ethics, the doctrine, the dogma, and the truth of the Holy Bible, and accept in heart, mind, and spirit that which God and Christ have put before you as the right way to live.

It bears repeating what is written in I Corinthians 2:12, 13, and 14, "Now we have received not the spirit of the world, but the spirit which is of God; that we might know the things that are freely giving us of God. This verse needs to be reflected on for a moment in consideration of what it means. We take for granted a good many things, but think about these things that were guaranteed by God, and yet, are being taken away from you by man.

By the very fact that you were born of God, and sent to earth by God, you are to be afforded a space on earth in which to live. This is being usurped by man by man's decision to control who may or may not live on the planet, and this is evident in the abortion issue, killing of others by murder, and even in the parameters of war, starvation, disease, and other ways of destroying people. Each person has the right to exist, and this is granted by God, but within the narrow confines which are being installed today, others will decide who has the right to exist on the planet. This idea and concept is based that individuals are in the "survival of the fittest mode, and therefore whosoever is in the way, can be blown away either physically, financially, or spiritually. The operational agenda is seen in the many slayings occurring in the public schools, where students rebel violently against ridicule, molestation, or torment by others. Without the regimen, ethics, and spiritual control put forth in the Holy Bible being taught to the students, and inasmuch they are taught they are animals living only this physical life, where then can there condemnation of their acts? If there is no judgment after death, then why worry about any consequences on earth?

Why has man become so ignorant that he cannot recognize that what the youth of today need is spiritual guidance and spiritual values, and that these traits cannot come from the teaching of atheism? All civility, all manner of good can only come from belief in God, and judgment in the life after death. If man is taught he is an animal, as science, education, government, and commerce wishes him to believe, then there is no life after death, and good works net nothing, but evil works bring temporary pleasure. Man continually believes man is good, but that isn't the truth any more than man is an animal. The only good in man comes from God, and if God is absent from our daily life, there is no good in anything we do. Why do you suppose there are so many people in jail today? They have run afoul of the law, but those laws were first put into effect by Christian and Godly thinking, and it is totally unfair to level Christian beliefs on animal behavior. If you want people to be Godly, you have to teach them to be Godly, and this means from the cradle upward. Who could prosecute a bull in court for goring a man? By the same token, if children are animals why should they be required to live to a code of ethics they are not taught before hand? To tell a child he is an animal, but that he must disobey his instincts in favor of ideals, is to ask the goring bull to abide by the same ethics. Do you really believe he will listen?

It is only when a child is taught that he is more than an animal, a unique creation by God, and in the image and likeness of God, that the child can accept the idealism and the ethics of choice. It is only then they can began to visualize and accept the concept of right and wrong. Does a goring bull know he is doing wrong? Neither can a child ascertain he is doing wrong if he hasn't been previously taught what is acceptable, and what is not. This is a function of spiritual belief and since it is spiritual, it is only effective if the child has been spiritually trained. A trained seal will perform tricks for a fish as a reward, but what is the reward of a child to do good, as compared to the short term pleasure he obtains by doing evil? If there is no God, there is no life after death, and there is no judgment, and no reason to do good works, especially since evil works do offer those short lived moments of pleasure.

Each person is afforded a space to occupy on earth as dictated by God bringing him to earth, and man needs to honor that inherited right. Along with this right is that a person, in being on the planet is entitled to a piece of ground upon which to dwell, raise food, and inhabit for his enjoyment and well being. Where is there a piece a land that is not owned by some person, government, or nation? Each person is entitled to a piece of ground, but isn't all the land on earth owned by someone other God? Think of it a moment. Each person on earth is entitled to a piece of land, but where does it say in the Bible a person must purchase this land from another person? Is not God the rightful owner and we the caretakers? The United States had the right idea of home steading where each person desiring a place to live was afforded the opportunity to have a piece of land, but that has long been abandoned in favor of the atheist greed of commerce, and government. There is no free land available to the generations being born, and it will soon come to pass that only land held by generations in the same family, will survive for some time. In the end, one gigantic corporation will own all land, and all things on the planet, and the individual will work for his bread and keep, whatever the final authority desires to give the individual. Is that really the way people want to live? It may not be, but it is coming shortly.

Each person is to have clean water to drink, and this is rapidly coming to a close. Most governments own all the fresh water, and to tap into this water supply, a person must pay a fee, and receive permission to drill a well. This is really evident in the squabble between the Federal Government, and the state government in the state of Washington concerning what has happened in the Columbia basin. The reclamation (irrigation of the desert land) from water of the Columbia river for the past fifty or more years has resulted in a vast aquifer under several counties, and the battle is over who owns this water. All that can be said is that, "The greed goes on!

The shortage of fresh water is starting to take shape today, and the pollution from farming and industry has made much of the fresh water on the planet undrinkable for some time to come. Filtration systems work partially, and this gives the semblance of everything being okay, but it isn't. As the climate and weather patterns change, as they are doing this very day, less water is going to be available, and alternate sources, such as desalting stations on the oceans will have to be employed to relieve the overuse of natural fresh water. Not one city in ten in the United States today has water pure enough to drink right from the tap.

Who isn't aware that we need clean pure air to breath? Look at what has happened to the atmosphere we breath. Acid rains, smog, and unwholesome emissions are becoming bigger problems as third world nation take over manufacturing products, which have been discontinued in nations such as the United States because strict air pollution standards could not be met by the factories. It seems the answer was reasoned, if we can't meet the air quality standards here, we'll go where there aren't any restrictions. Has anyone ever reasoned out that poisoning the air in Africa is just as deadly as poisoning the air in America? It doesn't appear so.

These inalienable rights given man by God, are slowly being surrendered into man's control, and the evidence is very plain for all to see. Just try to find something that isn't regulated by some form of government. Is this really freedom? Is this really liberty?

There is the argument that controls have to be put on for all to have benefit, but isn't it more reasonable to train people to respect God, his planet, and his people? If everyone lived the golden rule, would there be need for so many laws, regulations, ordinances, and rules? The ultimate is that people have to be trained into accepting the right way of life, and that can only come about by modifying the philosophy to accepting only the absolute truth, and the belief in God.

All men are to be spiritual. Read again the truth written in Isaiah 45:23, "1 have sworn by myself, the word is gone out of my mouth in righteousness, and shall not return, That unto me every knee shall bow, every tongue shall swear.

The old kick about there being a separation between church and state is plain nonsense. If you believe in God, that belief is going to be seen in everything thing you do, and if you do not believe in God, that belief will also be reflected in your behavior. There is no other way. You cannot in all good conscience say you are a Christian or Godly, and enact secular or atheist laws, and an atheist cannot in good conscience enact laws pertaining to Godly or Christian behavior. They are opposites, and cannot come to any reasonable coexistence of one with the other.

There neither can be an equality established between such divergent beliefs, so practicality speaks this about a nation. A nation formed and operated under Christian and Godly ethics is unsuitable to the atheist, and a nation founded on secular or atheism is unsuitable for those believing in God and Christ. Obviously there is going to be tension throughout the strata of such a mixed society, and this is what is occurring in the United States, and other Christian nations today. It must come to pass, either the Christian and God fearing people will rule, or the atheist will rule, for there is no in between ground. The same is true for the people of Israel. If they are to follow the dictates of other nations, and make concessions to the Palestinians, then they are again doomed to enslavement.

Understanding how each international incident, each national law enacted, or every policy instituted by the national leaders affects the individual is part of the important criteria of evaluating a person's future. This is becoming most critical as we move toward the end time, where incidents and events will occur in a rapid fire order, rather than long drawn out affairs. Because of this we are warned in Matthew 24:41, "Therefore be ye also ready: for in such an hour as ye may think not the Son of man cometh.

The practical side of the argument as to what to do, and how to begin can be summed up in a broad statement. It is written in Matthew 18:3, "And said, Verily I say unto you, Except ye be converted, and become as little children, ye shall not enter into the kingdom of heaven.

215

When Christ uttered these words, he was comparing man to young children, and several different things come forth from the understanding. A young child is totally dependent on his parents for guidance, sustenance, and safety, and this is the adaptation man must make to be converted to being Christ like. If we do not put our faith, trust, and reliance in Christ, then we are not child like. A person must shed the desire to proceed through life, making decisions, a living, and his personal welfare based upon worldly examples, and surrender to letting Christ guide the way in all things. The Lord is the shepherd and we are his sheep, and the sheep do not go where they wish, but where the shepherd leads them. It is a simple thing to understand the world's way is the wrong way, but it is also difficult in this day and age to escape the clutches of the world's influence. Despite the rhetoric, despite the fanfare, and despite the illusion painted by men, the only right way is the Lord's way, and until a person accepts that as the absolute truth, nothing good can happen in the way to salvation.

Starting with the trust possessed only by small children isn't an easy task for someone raised in this chaotic world. The whole world is shot through with deception, misunderstanding, and wrong interpretation about God, man, and the coming world. Until this dilemma is resolved, and until man changes his philosophy to be based solely on the absolute truth, salvation cannot come about. This is why it is important to revert back to trusting Christ and God for all things, being dependent upon him as a small child is to his parents. This doctrine may seem way off base, but the truth in the Holy Bible is not wavered by the ifs, ands, and buts, found in man's theories of how to live life.

Consider for just a moment the question, How many people fast and pray daily or weekly, monthly or yearly to secure God's favor? We are told and shown by example in the Holy Bible that prayer and fasting is one way to get God's attention to our needs, and yet few to none use the procedure. Most are given to the man made belief that God helps those who help themselves, which is a false doctrine.

If God is our Father, and we are his children, isn't it then logical that he's going to provide us with guidance, sustenance, and safety?

Part of the plan for salvation is learning to trust in God and Christ for the things we need, and Christ emphasized this in Matthew 7: 7 and 8, "Ask, and it shall be given you; seek, and ye shall find; knock, and it shall be opened unto you: For everyone that asketh receiveth, and he that seeketh findeth; and to him that knocketh it shall be opened. It cannot be said any more clearly than that.

The next major thing that has to occur is written in Matthew 10:32 and 33, "Whosoever there fore shall confess me before men, him will I confess also before my Father which is in heaven. But whosoever shall deny me before men, him will I also deny before my Father which is in heaven. This is the critical feature of salvation which neither the Judaic or Islamic religions will accept, and for that reason the people under these religions will be judged on their works alone, without the saving grace of Jesus Christ.

This is a tough road to go down, because each person in these two religions is banking on the fact they have done enough good in the world to be saved. How many do you suppose can enter the day of judgment secure in the knowledge they will be saved?

The baptizing of a person, which is the sealing of a person to Christ, is another requirement for conversion. John the Baptist came preaching and baptizing, saying the words written in Matthew 3:11, "I indeed baptize you with water unto repentance: but he that cometh after me is mightier than I, whose shoes I am not worthy to bear: he shall baptize you with the Holy Ghost, and with fire.

Jesus came to John and asked him to baptize him, and in Matthew 3:14 is recorded, "But John forbade him, saying, I have need to be baptized of thee, and comest thou to me?

In verse 15 Christ responds, "Suffer it to be so now: for thus it becometh us to fulfill all righteousness. It can be seen that Christ in his purity was baptized into belief in God, and into the mission he was to perform on earth. Why John did the baptism is revealed in Matthew 12, 13, and 14, "And from the days of John the Baptist until now the kingdom of heaven suffereth violence, and the violent take it by force. For all the prophets and the law prophesied until John. And if ye will receive it, this is Elias, which was for to come. In the understanding of this message it is that John is spiritually Elias. The key for the Judaic and the Islamic spiritual leaders to understand and preach is what Christ said in Matthew 17:11, 12, and 13, "And Jesus answered and said unto them, Elias shall first come, and restore all things. But I say unto you, That Elias is come already, and they knew him not, but have done unto him whatsoever they listed, likewise shall also the Son of man suffer of them. Then the disciples understood that he spake unto them of John the Baptist.

Baptism by a Christian is then part of the conversion of a person toward salvation. John the Baptist who spiritually is Elias, came eating locusts and honey, and the world thought he was a mad man, but he was only a man carrying out God's work. It's really no different today, a person dedicated to Christ and in pursuit of doing God's work on earth are looked upon by the rest of society as being a little "tetched in the head. Isaiah, Moses, John the Baptist, Abraham, Noah, Joseph, and all the men in the Holy Bible display the single outstanding trait, that of being a little eccentric as noted by the rest of society. Why this is should be readily recognized, because it speaks loud and clear that man isn't headed in the right direction, and God sends these different leaders, to correct man's pathway, even though they aren't heeded or taken seriously. The modern day disciple, the modern day evangelist, the modern day minister of Christ and God has the same trait as the men of the Holy Bible, and if they do not, they cannot be of God and Christ. The ways of God and Christ are alien to the ways of man, and it comes down to the same point, if you serve man, you may not be serving God, but if you serve God, you will be serving man as well.

For the conversion there must then be a reversion to being like a child, dependent upon the Father for all things, there must be a public acknowledgment of Christ as the Savior, and as your God, and there must be a baptism into the faith of Christ, in order to receive the Holy Ghost as your Instructor and Comforter. Without these three essential elements the conversion to Christian belief isn't possible in the average person. It must furthermore be recognized that in the acceptance and doing the three essential conversion elements, the person becomes dead to the world of man, and born into the world of spirituality as a new person. Word of this is in Romans 8: 10, "And if Christ be in you, the body is dead because of sin; but the Spirit is life because of righteousness.

It has to be emphasized again and again that the world has become deceived, and each individual must come to his senses and recognized that each person is deceived a certain amount, some more than other, and each person has to strive toward replacing that which is wrong in their philosophy, with what is right and the truth. It begins with simple truths, and progresses toward the spectrum of righteous knowledge of the holy, and the truth about all things.

The new Christian isn't blessed with total consummation right off, but must continue to extend his education toward God and Christ, and the understanding of their ways. This can only be accomplished by reading the Holy Bible and letting the Holy Ghost instruct you as to the meaning. The world will beat a pathway to your door, not in support of your new life, but to dissuade and discourage you from your quest for the absolute truth. It can be said that misery likes company, and they don't want you to escape from world of misery.

It is at this time a new Christian has to seek the strength and fortifying presence of God and Christ, because these first new convictions (that of changing from a worldly status to a spiritual status) are easy disrupted by old habits and old beliefs. One of the most beneficial goals to think of during these times, is the day when you will share the kingdom of heaven on earth in immortality and in the presence of God and Christ. What greater thing can be enjoyed than to be elevated to such a height in glory and stature?

There remains before all mankind, the question of why God made so many galaxies, suns, and planets if they were not to be inhabited, and the answer is probably a little simpler than a person might suppose. It would seem feasible and logical, that in the beginning when God decided to replicate himself in the form of man, he had in mind that man was to be his children, and as his children, man would be little Gods. It appears that God, innately has the desire for a kingdom to rule over, and man, being the offspring of God, seems also to have that innate quality, but is unable to utilize it righteously at the present. It is obvious that Eve more or less threw a monkey wrench into the works by interrupting God's tutelage of Adam and herself by eating of the fruit of the tree of knowledge, before God was ready for them to do so.

It isn't too far out to believe that when God laid out the pattern of the Universe, that he considered the question that if man were to be in his own image and likeness, all mankind would then be little Gods, and as such would bear the innate quality of wanting a realm to rule over. God's first attempt at teaching Adam to be a little God, was through assigning everything on earth to his care, and making him superior over all other species of life on the planet.

The facts are echoed out by how man has not utilized the planet's resources wisely, but has been wantonly brutish and wasteful. This behavior testifies that man is not ready to assume his rightful place in God's government over the kingdom. The pattern of the Universe was evidently set up so that each person, under God, could have powers of a sub God, over perhaps a galaxy or over a solar system.

It cannot be argued logically that God needed all the different bodies in the Universe to produce earth and man, and that leads to the conclusion there had to be another reason. Another part of the equation is that when the people finally reach the point in time, where they live in God's light with God the Father, God the Son, and God the Holy Ghost, what are they to do as works? Service, adoration, and worship of God as a constant duty doesn't fulfill the basic innate need of God or man to have a kingdom. From the view that man might someday be elevated to a Godly position over different parts of the Universe, under God, meets both regimens. This is fairly well documented in the case of the Son of God being the Inheritor of the kingdom. Jewish law held the eldest son received the birth right, even as Esau received the birthright over Jacob his twin brother, because he was born first.

In maintaining the law and the order of descendants Christ is given control over all the kingdom, and the other children of God, mankind, would receive lesser kingdoms for their inheritance. This would mean each person is to have some type of kingdom, and that his rule over such a kingdom would be in accordance to Christ's rule. This also means where Christ is elevated as a God over all the kingdom, and man is elevated to the level of being a lesser God. Why we are to be a lesser God is because we are part of God through Christ, and a part can never equal the whole of anything. Christ being one entity of God is above man, but Christ alone is not God in total, because there is also the Father, and the Holy Ghost. Man is therefore

221

relegated a position of some control in the kingdom, but on a lesser level of Christ, and lesser yet to God.

This concept is partly borne out by fact that in the last part of Revelation, concerning the great city Jerusalem, there is no mention of angels, as there are in the previous chapters. The spoken word is about man's relationship to Christ and God, and there has to be a wonderment as to what happened to the angels? In the model put forth here, it is by what is written in Revelation 22:12, that some support is received that man may replace the angels as administrators of God's creation. "And, behold, I come quickly; and my reward is with me, to give to every man according as his work shall be.

Considering that science tells us there are countless billions of galaxies, solar systems, and planets, and given that man was created in the image and likeness of God, and with the innate trait of wanting to be like a God, it seems justified that God prepared the way to fulfill his desire, and the desire of his offspring, mankind.

As in today's life, there are the leaders of society, and there are nations who lead the other nations, and this can be applied to a person ruling over a planet, and another person ruling over a whole solar system, and another over a galaxy and so on. There is no way to determine how many people have lived upon the earth from the beginning, nor is there a way to determine how many are going to proceed through the different phases to become as a little God. Surely the desire to be as a little God exists in each person, and it's expressed by the saying, "If I were God ....

There has been the age old question of why God lets so much brutality, pain, sickness, strife, worry, and contention exist in the world, and it is part of the training session to elevate man toward his rightful position in God's hierarchy. It should be obvious that those inflicting upon mankind the atrocities found in the world, aren't going to advance past this life we are now living. Those who attend to the business of studying God's words, and applying the lessons learned through the Holy Ghost, are going to continue to advance to the next level of training.

This training can be looked at as having three grades or level of learning. The life here on earth is the kindergarten, where we are supposed to learn how to get along with one another, and begin to understand the rudimentary elements of becoming a God. The next level, is the time on earth when Christ returns to earth, and a judgment is rendered on each person to determine their fitness to do one of two things. Either a person is resurrected to live a thousand years under Christ's rule to learn how to live in peace and harmony, or else the person remains in the waiting room for the thousand years to pass, without receiving the benefit of being trained how to live in total peace and haony. This is why it is extremely important for each person to carefully weigh out every aspect of their life and make the needed adjustments right now while there is time.

It is obvious that if you fail the kindergarten training, you will not receive the training afforded under the thousand years of Christ's rule. Those failing the kindergarten phase will go into the second life with only the barest minimum of training, and quite possibly with only remembrance of hell's fire, the same as the rich man in the narrative of Lazarus and the rich man.

The second judgment is much harsher, and here those who fail are destroyed out of existence in the lake of fire. Those who successfully pass the kindergarten stage, advance through the thousand year reign with Christ, and those who do not succumb to Satan's wiles prior to the second judgment, will proceed into immortality, and a status of being a child of God.

It should be clear that life itself is a test, and if we do not prepare for it, we are going to fail. There is no way we can wait to the last moments, and then cram for the test. It has to be done by everyday study, everyday day application, and through every day asking God to aid us in the quest to become worthy of being a child of God. This is no time to try to copy from your neighbors work, but it is the time to undertake the serious endeavor to read, and digest all that is written in the Holy Bible.

Man dreams of the day when he can leave earth and travel to distant planets, and this epitomizes the innate trait of wanting to be like God. The problem is that man hasn't yet progressed from the kindergarten level, because he has failed to accept the truth, the instruction, and the wisdom afforded him through God, Christ, and the Holy Ghost. We neither read nor capitulate to what is written in the Holy Bible, and we didn't listen or heed what we were told by God and Christ. The inability of man to rid himself of being "stiff necked toward instruction, and his gullibility toward doing that which is wrong, keeps man from progressing to the next level. How can God trust us to manage a solar system when we can't manage ourselves on earth?

Like Satan, man has deceived himself into believing he can be like God, without further training or knowledge, and that's a rather stupid way of proceeding, especially since God has laid out the pathway clearly marked for us to travel. It has to make a person wonder why man is so prevalent to travel on a path fraught with quicksand when there is a paved road to follow?

The reward of living a Godly and Christian life are many, but the single most important reward is that it allows a person to graduate from the kindergarten level into the level of living on earth during Christ's thousand year reign. It also places an individual to be better equipped when the Tempter (Satan) is allowed access to man again to deceive him again. Finally, the prudent person is going to share immortality with God and Christ, and this is the ultimate desire of all people, to be like God himself.

The argument put forth in the text has been to bring clarity to an otherwise chaotic mess found in the world today. It takes years to sort out each question and there is no one particular answer short of yea or nay that can portray every event that has or will take place. The general way has been set, and God has been kind enough to send Christ to lead the way to immortality, and it is now up to mankind to determine individually and severally whether or not to follow God's way. It is a very simple choice, it is either to eternal life or to destruction in the lake of fire. Each person has to make their choice wisely, and each nation must set their pattern of being a servant either to God or to Satan. There is no other alternative.

These are the important things to consider when you step into the voter's booth the next time. The selection is easy. Is this candidate for God or for Satan? The only criteria you have to go on, is what the candidate says, but does his past record indicate the same?

The powers to be (under Satan) demand partisanship, because they cannot afford to let the mind of the people freely choose the right person for the job, in accordance with God's agenda for the nation.

The United States, Britain, and the other Christian nations stand at the open doorway with the power, majesty, and rightful duty to establish God's way throughout the world with God's blessing, but the challenge is no longer being accepted by these great nations, and means God will withdraw his strength, majesty and power, and will let Satan have his way with them. This means the individual Christian is to suffer more for not maintaining the heritage God installed in these free nations. What is happening to Israel today, is going to happen also, and has already begun, in nations like the United States. The days of peace, prosperity, and happiness are to vanish like smoke in the air, and it is because we have abandoned God. It is wrong to think God has abandoned man, because the truth is man has abandoned God in pursuit of evil instead of righteousness. Until that truth is learned, nothing more can be learned.

One of the most intriguing questions is whether the Christian nations of the world will reverse their current path toward honoring Satan, and return to God's guidance and care, or suffer the consequences of their actions, the same as Adam and Eve caused the suffering of mankind by their ignoring God's advice and directions? The answer is gloomy, because God already knows that mankind is headed toward total enslavement under Satan, and won't reverse their course until Christ comes again to rescue them. A person has to wonder why man is unable to see the errors of his ways, alter his course, toward God and away from evil?

It has been explained that individuals make up the population of the world, and individuals form the government of every nation, and individuals form the family unit, the building blocks of society, and from this understanding it has to be recognized that each individual contributes to what the family, nation, and world does as a whole. There is good sense in saying that democracy, liberty, and freedom must be protected to be preserved, and that requires each individual give freely of his mind and talents to assure a society under the three main attributes continue. Apathy, avoidance of duty, and desertion of God's ways and doctrine leads only to enslavement of the worse kind.

The only way the present trend of the people on earth can be reversed is by educating children toward the merits and advantage of being Godly and not Satanic. Public schools, public meetings, and every home should be God and Christ centered. This does not violate any person's right to believe the way they wish, but it does insure the nation's ability to remain free.

If an atheist wishes to ignore the Christian prayer to God, common courtesy of civilization requires the person to remain silent in respect for unity in the society. It is rude to interrupt someone speaking to another person, and it is rude to speak to someone speaking silently to God in prayer. The same is true between religions, even though the religion may be wrong. A Christian does not have to join a prayer to an idol or other foreign deity, and the Christian may either remain silent, or pray to God during the moment. Who then should be offended by a prayer? The law may stipulate a separation between church and state, but that is to say no church is to be recognized as the national ideal of church. The individual right to pray to God at any hour of the day or night cannot be legislated, because a silent prayer is just as effective as a prayer spoken aloud. One of the greatest illustrations of how prayer is used by a Christian is written in Acts 7:60, where Stephen is stoned to death. "And he kneeled down, and cried in a loud voice, Lord lay not this sin to their charge. And when he had said this, he fell asleep. The verse demonstrates the fervor of belief in God and Christ, by Stephen, and illustrates how God lifts a devoted person away from pain and suffering. Does anyone believe they can have such fervent love for God and Christ? In the end we all do because we surrender ourselves to physical death in favor of spiritual life. This is the act we call dying.

The world has made remarkable achievements in every aspect of life and learning except when it comes to God and Christ, and there the world has let itself become deceived with inaccurate and false information. The establishment of untruth in man's philosophy can only lead to discouragement and peril, whereas the truth brings the safety of the light. The reflection, "I have seen the light! is more than a statement of receiving the truth about any given subject. It is also the internal light of satisfaction one feels when they know for sure they are right. Our entire body responds with positive rather than negative responses. It can be as simple as being able to answer faultlessly a question posed by a teacher or instructor as a test question, and the good feeling the student feels when he knows his answer was text book correct. The same feeling is derived when a person approaches to Christ, and amends his ways of living to Christ's standards. This doesn't mean to wear long robes and long hair as the men of that day did, but it means to live in the spirit and intent of what Christ would do in the same situation.

There is a time to speak out, and there is a time to remain silent. In all things, the Christian is allowed to use Christ's words to every occasion, but in the correct content and intent. By doing this, the Christian is teaching as well as providing sound advice or instruction to another or group. An example is when someone does something mean to you, and you respond with the words, "May God rebuke you. This is not spiteful on your part, but in compliance to what God and Christ teach. To the person, it requires them to think about their actions, or words, and how God would also look at them? In this way a simple statement has a profound effect, and by using Christ's words in our everyday language betters all concerned.

It has been shown that God is Alpha and Omega, the beginning and end, the first and the last. It has been demonstrated how a person can determine God actually exists, and it has been shown how the Universe, earth and man was created by God to inherit with Christ the kingdom of God. Some light has been shed on how the basic truth of the Holy Bible should be lived, and promoted throughout the world if we are to be the servants and disciples of Christ and God. Using plain old common sense is shown to be the best way to proceed through life, using the handbook of life, the Holy Bible, as the authoritative reference. Finally, there has been enough evidence submitted to encourage each individual to develop his own personal philosophy using only the absolute truth of the Holy Bible as its foundation belief. "Hearken unto me, ye that know righteousness, the people in whose heart is my law; fear ye not the reproach of men, neither be ye afraid of their reviling. For the moth shall eat them up like a garment, and the worm shall eat them like wool: but my righteousness shall be for ever, and my salvation from generation to generation.

The End